THE
WASHINGTON NATIONALS
1859 TO TODAY

THE
WASHINGTON NATIONALS
1859 TO TODAY

The Story of Baseball in the Nation's Capital

To the D.C. Public Library
I couldn't have done this book without you!

FREDERIC J. FROMMER

TAYLOR TRADE PUBLISHING
Lanham • Boulder • New York • Toronto • Oxford

Published by Taylor Trade Publishing
An imprint of The Rowman & Littlefield Publishing Group, Inc.
4501 Forbes Boulevard, Suite 200, Lanham, Maryland 20706

Distributed by NATIONAL BOOK NETWORK

Library of Congress Cataloging-in-Publication Data

Frommer, Frederic J.
   The Washington Nationals 1859 to today : the story of baseball in the nation's capital / Frederic J. Frommer. — 1st Taylor Trade Pub. ed.
      p. cm.
   Includes bibliographical references.
   ISBN 1-58979-273-4 (cloth : alk. paper)
   1. Baseball—Washington (D.C.)—History. 2. Washington Senators (Baseball team : 1886–1960) 3. Washington Senators (Baseball team : 1961–1971) 4. Washington Nationals (Baseball team)   I. Title.
GV863.W18F76 2006
796.357'64'09753—dc22   2005024353

∞™ The paper used in this publication meets the minimum requirements of American National Standard for Information Sciences—Permanence of Paper for Printed Library Materials, ANSI/NISO Z39.48-1992.

Manufactured in the United States of America.

CONTENTS

CONTENTS

TEN

PREFACE

When I moved to Washington in 1998, I found two things lacking in this city: a place to get a good slice of pizza and a baseball team.

In the summer of 2004, I followed the District's bid to land the Montreal Expos as closely as any pennant race. I was elated when Major League Baseball awarded the team to Washington, and even more so when I got a chance to write a book about the history of baseball in the nation's capital.

As a lifelong baseball fan, I knew all about the two versions of the Washington Senators, how the city lost the team in 1961 and then gave the same name to the team that took its place. This chronology always struck me as kind of strange. Sure, some cities have had two teams in different sports with the same name – St. Louis had the baseball and football Cardinals, and before that, New York had the baseball and football Giants. But in Washington's case, it seemed like the city was trying to maintain the illusion of one franchise all along.

Bad idea. The old Senators were coming off seven consecutive losing seasons, and the new Senators picked up the torch by finishing under .500 for eight straight years. With that track record, many fans were reluctant to see a third franchise with the jinxed Senators nickname, so the city and Major League Baseball chose the "Nationals" instead. But this, too, was a throwback name, because Washington's baseball team was officially known as the Nationals until 1956, although many fans called them the Senators.

Now that the city finally had a new baseball team, would they have much of a following in a city of transplants? Vice President Dick Cheney had it backward when he said: "It will force a lot of us to reorient our loyalties. We've all picked up, acquired, become fans of other teams."

Many Washingtonians, in fact, had brought their rooting interests with them from other cities, not picked them up while living in the District. These fans faced a dilemma: did they owe their loyalty to their original teams, or to their new home?

A native New Yorker living in Washington, *New York Times* columnist David Brooks, admitted he was thinking of switching allegiances from the Mets to the newborn team, calling his affection for the Nats "the love that dare not speak its name."

"In the midst of this spiritual crisis I have begun to ask the fundamental question," Brooks wrote. "What is the nature of the loyalty that binds us to our teams? Can a team be tossed aside even though it has given you (especially during the 1970s) some of the worst years of its life?"

Indeed, many local fans did abandon their original hometown teams, a task made easier by the Nats' ridiculously successful first half, when they catapulted to first place. But the Nats also faced a fairly high percentage of enemy fans at their games, a product, no doubt, of the thousands of local fans who stayed with the team that brought them to the sport. This was especially the case when the New York Mets and Chicago Cubs came to town.

What does it mean to be a fan? Is rooting interest inextricably linked to one's city? If so, does that loyalty stay with a fan's original town, or does it transfer to the fan's new city? Or is rooting a lifelong commitment to one team, even one selected on a childhood whim because of an affinity for a bird or color? Native Washingtonians also faced this dilemma, unless they had ignored the sport until 2005.

Two groups of fans didn't face these existential questions. The old-time Senators fans waited patiently for baseball to return. Sure, they may have had casual relationships with the Orioles or some other team, but these veteran Washingtonians were just biding their time.

The other group: fans too young to have selected a team before the Expos came to town. These newborn baseball fans got the perfect twofer in 2005: a new sport to root for, and a new hometown team to go along with it.

Frederic J. Frommer
November, 2005
Washington, D.C.

FOREWORD

ANTHONY WILLIAMS, WASHINGTON, D.C., MAYOR

One of the most exciting moments in my life took place last spring, when I was called upon to throw out the first pitch in the team's first game in RFK Stadium. Walking out onto the field, the sky a stunning blue, the grass a beautiful green and the stands awash in red and white, I was overcome by the excitement and joy felt for this team, for this sport.

It was a long time coming bringing baseball back to our nation's capital. But at that moment, the long struggle seemed worth every bit of effort.

There are few places in America where baseball is more appropriately a part of the fabric of the city than here in Washington, D.C.

I say that to people all the time and I'm often struck by their responses: surely New York, Boston, Chicago or even Los Angeles—my home town—are more passionate baseball towns than Washington. Fans say those cities are teaming with diehard supporters, colorful narratives and years of tradition. Even St. Louis, home of the Cardinals, is steeped in a century of deep-seated baseball lore—none more vivid than the lady who once looked at her team and remarked: "What a lovely shade of Cardinal," christening the team with its evocative name.

But Washington is a unique city.

It's here that the best intentions of our country are played out each day, in the disorderly process of governing. The rhythm of the Congress, the White House and the courts are all intertwined with the atmosphere of the District, which always tends to feel a little more laid back in the summer when elected officials return to their home states and the city's residents have the place to themselves. Those summer nights, where the crickets are chirping and our iconic monuments are bathed in light, cry out for the roar of a crowd at a languid baseball game.

More to the point, for those that argue that baseball represents the optimism and idealism of our country, it's perfect that those virtues are housed here in the District of Columbia, home of the president and Congress.

Just as our city bursts forth each year with cherry blossoms and good intentions, baseball teams approach spring as a coming together of teammates from varied backgrounds with high hopes for the epic struggle facing them. It's a journey, reborn each year.

Of course, it's a bitter irony that here within the city's borders, the people who live and work here, who go off to war and pay their taxes, who watch baseball and raise families, are denied the most basic right—a vote in Congress. We continue to pursue that goal, even as our city welcomes baseball back after a 33-year absence.

The return of the team, played out in 2005 at a refurbished RFK Stadium, is also a telling emblem of the city's return to greatness and continued renaissance.

The optimism and enthusiasm that surrounded the Nationals' first season back in D.C. is just one part of the broader spirit of hopefulness that we are attempting to again make part of our city. Although our city remains a work in progress, we've come miles forward in terms of providing good housing, jobs and opportunities for the people who live here. Bringing the Nationals to our city is like landing a major corporation—from the new jobs provided by the organization and new stadium construction to the millions in new investments that the presence of the team has sparked along the great Anacostia River. In fact, our broader plan for the Nationals includes making the rundown warehouses and abandoned buildings that dot the waterfront into a sparkling gem, a destination where people of all backgrounds can come together over baseball.

For many years, the District was blessed to have the Senators play their games near the center—and the soul—of the city, Griffith Stadium near Howard University.

My hope is that not only will a new ballpark revitalize South Capitol Street, creating a new lively corner of the city that can help bridge the divide between East and West Washington. We need to span the gap that still separates one side of the Anacostia from the other.

All of this contributes toward moving the city forward.

During the city's public debate over the merits of the stadium plan, I often found myself caught in the middle of two immovable forces: the council and Major League Baseball.

They could not be more unlike one another, and each was determined to protect its interests to the last day. In the end, we were able to pull together a deal that provides a stadium that the city owns, paid for not with general revenue but primarily with a special tax on large businesses and additional fees on concessions and by the team itself. It marked a good compromise, given the tough realities of professional sports in this age.

My hope is that in time, the new stadium will pump enough new benefits into our community that opponents of bringing the team to Washington will come to see why it was the right thing to do.

In the meantime, we are looking forward to next season. All true baseball fans are eternal optimists and I'm no exception. I watched the Nationals adjust to their new home and new fans beginning in the spring and continuing into the glorious span in summer, when they were briefly in first place. Other teams caught up by fall, but we all saw the heart of a great team on the field and I know there remains a lot of enthusiasm for a local team.

People ask if returning baseball to our nation's capital will be the starting point for my legacy. To me, it's inextricably linked to the broader improvements we've brought about citywide.

ONE

BEGINNINGS

ONE

BEGINNINGS

The Montreal Expos moved to Washington in 2005 as wards of the state. Major League Baseball owned the vagabond franchise, deciding the team's fate, from how much it spent to where it played. Nationals fans may have seethed over the outside control, but the arrangement actually mirrored Washington's first modern-era team a century earlier.

When the American League started play in 1901, league president Ban Johnson controlled 51 percent of every team, including the original Washington Nationals, known more popularly as the Senators. Two years later, the league tightened its grip over the infant Washington franchise by buying out team president Fred Postal's stock. Only in 1904 did the team finally have independent ownership, when a group including Thomas C. Noyes, whose family published the *Washington Star*, bought the team.

Although 1901 marked the beginning of the city's first lasting franchise, Washington baseball went back at least 40 years before. In 1859, a group of government clerks formed the "Potomacs," winning this approving description from the *Washington Star*: "It is good to see health-promoting exercises taking the place of insipid enervating amusements."

That same year, other government workers started up the National Base Ball Club of Washington, D.C., or "Nationals." The team included Arthur Pue Gorman, a 21-year-old pitcher who went on to become a U.S. senator and the inspiration for the name Washington Senators.

The club's constitution still exists today at the Washington Historical Society, laying out the club's bylaws. Players were required to pay a 50-cent initiation fee and monthly dues of 25 cents. The members were mostly government clerks—upper-middle-class gentlemen—and they envisioned a gentlemen's game. As such, there would be fines for anti-social behavior: 10 cents for "profane or improper language," 25 cents for disputing an umpire's call, even a 10-cent fine for expressing an opinion on a close call before the umpire made his decision.

Such fines would wipe out today's players, even at those rates.

On May 5, 1860, six months before Abraham Lincoln was elected president, the Nationals and Potomacs squared off for a game on the "White Lot," a field near the White House now known as the Ellipse, where recreational softball games are played today. The score was like a softball game, with the Potomacs winning 35–15, thanks to rules that allowed a batter to dictate where the pitch would be thrown. A month later, the Nationals avenged the loss with a 46–14 victory. And so a friendly rivalry was born.

Newspaper accounts of the games between the Nationals and Potomacs offer a glimpse of the gentlemanly game envisioned by the Nationals' constitution. One story notes: "The game was witnessed by a large number of spectators, including nearly four hundred ladies, representing the beauty and fashion of the capital."

Apparently, both teams had developed something of a home-field advantage, although neither one wanted to acknowledge it. The Nationals played on Capitol Hill, while the Potomacs called the White Lot their home. Being able to win games away from "home" became a point of pride.

A newspaper story described the subtext:

"The Base Ball fraternity and the sympathizing public began to say that each club had the advantage on its own grounds; and the Potomacs, unwilling to admit this, yielded to the wish of the Nationals to play on their grounds the game deciding the championship of Washington, and probably the South." The Potomacs made their point. They won that late-October game, an ancient fall classic, 32–16, on the Nationals' home field.

"The result has been a triumph for the Potomac by more handsome odds than ever," this reporter added.

The piece provoked an angry response from both teams. A letter to the editor signed by "National" retorted that both teams had agreed ahead of time that whoever won the pre-game coin toss would choose to play on the opponents' field. A member of the Potomacs wrote in, too, saying his team had chosen to play on the Nationals' grounds after winning the coin toss "to disabuse the public of an idea which has gained credence that a club could play best on their own ground, and *not* for any other reason."

He also apologized for some of his teammates who "were betrayed into expressions of triumph, and disposed to be a little more boastful than either good taste or sober second thought would permit." One can assume there wasn't any trash-talking or high-fives, but celebrations didn't fit in with the game as it was played back then.

One of the first fans was President Lincoln. A November 1860 editorial cartoon shows him vanquishing his three opponents in the presidential race on a baseball diamond. Each candidate holds a bat with his political position: "fusion," "nonintervention," "slavery extension," and in Lincoln's case, "equal rights and free territory." The president-elect is standing on home plate.

THE NATIONAL GAME. THREE "OUTS" AND ONE "RUN".
ABRAHAM WINNING THE BALL.

This Currier and Ives cartoon from 1860 uses baseball as a metaphor for Abraham Lincoln's triumph over his opponents in his first presidential election. Library of Congress

The Potomacs, despite their "championship," soon faded from view, while the Nationals continued to play baseball through the Civil War. In the summer of 1865, they played a tournament against the Brooklyn Atlantics and Philadelphia Athletics at the Ellipse. Lincoln's successor, President Andrew Johnson, let government clerks out early to catch the action. (What a cool boss!) He attended one of the games himself, along with six thousand other fans.

The local team made a poor showing. The Nationals lost the first game, 87–12, to Philadelphia, and then fell to Brooklyn, 34–19. But the game continued to increase in social stature, as the players from all teams visited Johnson at the White House. In October, Washington took on another team from Brooklyn, the Excelsiors, and earned a matter of East Coast respect by beating them, 36–30. That night, the home team feted their guests with a "complimentary dinner" of mock turtle soup, baked bluefish with port wine sauce, boiled ham, tongue, leg of mutton with caper sauce, and other old-school entrees.

The rivalry with New York continued the next season. An 1866 newspaper story observed, "This game is becoming a matter of national importance. As New York is the centre of the fraternity of the North, Washington is the baseball city of the South." In fact, the Nationals' only losses in 1866 were in New York, according to "The Washington Nationals and the Development of America's National Pastime," a historical paper by Frank Ceresi and Carol McMains.

"As much of a mark as the Nationals had made in the capital region, even being dubbed 'champions of the South,' New York was still the baseball capital," they wrote.

Also in 1866, the Nationals accepted a challenge from the American Cricket Club. They smoked their bat-and-ball cousins, 70–10.

The following season, 1867, the Nationals took off on a tour of what was then considered the West—cities like Cincinnati, Louisville, Indianapolis, Chicago, and St. Louis. Winning big, the Nationals walloped opponents by margins such as 53–10, 88–12, and 90–10—before being upset by the Forest City Club of Rockford, Illinois, 29–23, their only loss of the trip. Washington rebounded by throttling the Chicago Excelsiors, 49–4.

The gentlemanly era of the sport was passing. In 1870, a poolroom owner named Mike Scanlon laid the groundwork for more organized baseball by building a ballpark at the corner of 17th and S Streets, N.W., complete with 500 seats.

His team, the Olympics, entered the National Association of Professional Baseball Players the following season, winning 16 of 31 games. The Nationals joined them in the league in 1872. But setting a pattern of Washington baseball futility, both teams finished at the bottom of the league—the Nationals last in the 11-team league, and the Olympics eighth.

The league disbanded in 1875, replaced by the National League of Professional Base Ball Clubs in 1876, which did not include a Washington franchise. But D.C. teams did make several appearances in the 1880s: the Washington Statesmen in the American Association, the Washington Nationals in the Union Association, and a four-year stint by the Washington Nationals in the National League. None of them were any good. The Nationals, for example, finished last three times in the eight-team National League, and seventh once, before hanging up their spikes after the 1889 season.

But the Nats did feature some notable players in their short big league run. One was Cornelius Alexander McGillicuddy, an excellent defensive catcher and fan favorite. Sportswriters shortened his name to Connie Mack, and the young catcher went on to make his mark as a Hall-of-Fame manager. He managed the Philadelphia Athletics an amazing 50 years, covering the first half of the 20th century.

In 1888, a deaf-mute player named William Hoy, known as "Dummy" Hoy, stole 82 bases as a rookie outfielder for Washington. According to legend, umpires began to use hand signals to accommodate his disability. Seventy-three years later, at the age of 99, he threw out the first ball of the 1961 World Series. His life story was turned into a play called *The Signal Season of Dummy Hoy*.

Visiting ballplayers in Hoy's days would stay at the downtown Willard Hotel, where they would sit in armchairs in front of the building, chew tobacco, and fraternize with fans on a street nicknamed "Boulevard de Base Ball." A *Washington Star* story described an interaction one day between player Mike Kelly and a local fan.

"Why is it that Washington can't win any pennant?" the fan asked.

"Because you are so damned busy making money in that place across the street," Kelly responded, pointing to the Treasury Building, "that you don't give time enough to the honest occupation of playing baseball right."

A new Washington team was admitted to an expanded twelve-team National League in 1892. Unfortunately, this early version of the Senators wasn't much better than its predecessors, finishing higher than ninth only once, and never playing over .500, in its eight years of existence.

The Senators were owned by a pair of brothers from Philadelphia, George and J. Earl Warner, who did little to advance baseball's cause in Washington. The National League bought out the Senators after the 1899 season, returning to eight teams again as the league also folded franchises in Louisville, Baltimore, and Cleveland. When Ban Johnson started the American League in 1901, Washington was given another chance. This new team was named the Nationals, to avoid confusion with the 1890s team, but fans would continue to refer to them as the Senators.

Washington got off to a bad start. It finished with a .459 winning percentage, sixth place in the eight-team league, blowing one game to Cleveland after leading 13–5 with two outs in the ninth inning. The team's luck would not improve any time soon. In 1902, Washington signed away outfielder Ed Delahanty from the Philadelphia Phillies of the rival National League, giving him a $1,000 bump in salary to $4,000. Coming off a .354 season for the Phillies, Delahanty was one of the best hitters in the game, and he turned it up a notch for the Senators in 1902, hitting a league-high .376. But just two months into the 1903 season, Delahanty, who drank heavily, was suspended for missing a game. He boarded a train from Detroit to New York and was ejected near Niagara Falls for threatening riders. His body was found a few days later in the Niagara River. He was 35.

That 1903 season Washington stumbled to a last-place finish, one of many, with a 43–94 record (.314). In 1904, the Nationals lost their first 13 games on their way to the franchise's worst season ever, 38–113 (.252), and another last-place finish. The team averaged only 1,689 fans a game that year, last in the American League. The team would finish no higher than seventh place until the 1912 season.

American League Park in Washington, May 6, 1905. About 9300 people are in attendance. Library of Congress

A turning point came in 1907. That season, manager Joe Cantillon sent the team's catcher, Cliff Blankenship, on a western scouting trip to check out some prospects. One was speedster Clyde Milan, who made the team that year and became the Senators' starting center fielder for the next decade and a half. The other was a young player pitching in Idaho who had come recommended by a traveling salesman.

Walter Perry Johnson, just 19 years old, impressed Blankenship immediately. "You can't hit what you can't see," the catcher telegraphed Cantillon. "I've signed him and he is on his way."

The Nationals acted just in time. The New York Highlanders' manager, Clark Griffith, had also gotten word from a friend in Idaho to check out the flame-throwing teenager. By the time Griffith wrote back to send Johnson to New York for a tryout, Washington had already signed him. It worked out well for Griffith, who took over the Senators a few years later.

Johnson was quickly labeled a can't-miss by Washington sportswriters. "SECURES A PHENOM," a *Washington Post* headline declared on June 30, 1907. A subhead explained, "Johnson His Name and He Hails from the Wooly West." The story reported that Johnson had pitched 75 scoreless innings in the semipro Idaho State League and averaged more than 15 strikeouts a game. Cantillon helped fuel the hype, perhaps tongue-in-cheek, by saying, "If this fellow is what they say he is we (will) have to use only two men in a game, a catcher and Johnson. He strikes out most of the men, so why have an infield and an outfield? I shall give all the boys but the catchers days off when Johnson pitches."

That was just barely hyperbole. Johnson posted a 1.88 ERA in 110 innings for the Senators that year. The team was so awful, finishing with a .325 winning percentage in 1907, that Johnson's pitching prowess was good for just a 5–9 record. But the "Big Train" was on his way. The next year, his first full season, Johnson managed to go 14–14 for another bad Senators team, this time with a 1.65 ERA. He "slumped" to a 2.22 ERA in 1909, the only time in his first 10 years with an ERA over 2.00.

Not only was Johnson an exceptional athlete, but he was an exception to one of sports' unfortunate truisms: arrogance and greatness go hand-in-hand. A nonsmoker and nondrinker, Johnson's strongest expression was "Goodness gracious sakes alive." He hated to hit batters; Ty Cobb admitted he took advantage of Johnson's good nature by crowding the plate, knowing Johnson would not brush him back.

Sportswriters nicknamed him "Sir Walter" and the "White Knight." Teammates called him "Barney," for the race car driver Barney Oldfield. Another of his many nicknames was "The Big Swede," even though Johnson hailed from German stock. But he never bothered to correct the record. "There are a lot of nice Swedish people, I guess," he said. "I don't want to offend anybody."

Hitters sure found him offensive. Once, Johnson blew two fastballs by Cleveland's Ray Chapman, and the batter started walking back to the dugout. When the umpire told him he had only two strikes, Chapman responded, "I know, and you can have the next one. It won't do me any good."

Folks also called Johnson the "Kansas Cyclone," playing off his birthplace of Humboldt, Kansas. Legend has it that he developed his pitching speed by pitching hay on the farm back in Kansas. Johnson wasn't your classic power pitcher. He actually threw more with a sidearm delivery and didn't mix in very many off-speed pitches. "Walter's idea of a changeup was to just throw harder," said Cobb, arguably the best hitter in baseball history.

"The first time I faced him, I watched him take that easy windup—and then something went past me that made me flinch," Cobb wrote in his book, *My Life in Baseball*. "I hardly saw the pitch, but I heard it. The thing just hissed with danger. Every one of us knew we'd met the most powerful arm ever turned loose in a ballpark."

William McCarty watched Johnson as a young fan.

"He had a windmill windup, and when he got through with it, he'd throw it as hard as anyone at the time," recalls McCarty, who became team mascot and ballboy in the early 1930s, when Johnson was manager. "But he was a very soft guy. He set a great example, telling me the things I needed to do to succeed in life."

Johnson set the all-time strikeout record of 3,508 (later broken by Nolan Ryan), and led the league in strikeouts a dozen times. His 417–279 record (.599) puts him second in career wins, behind Cy Young. He still holds the record for career shutouts, 110, which surely will never be matched in today's obsessive pitch count era. Once, he shut out the New York Highlanders (later renamed the Yankees) three times in four days. He probably could have thrown four shutouts, except that there was no Sunday baseball played back then in New York.

Johnson could do it all. In those days, when starting pitchers often came in to relieve on their days "off," Johnson went 40–30 with 34 saves out of the bullpen. He had a career batting average of .235, with 24 home runs, and hit an astonishing .433 one season.

*Walter Johnson, arguably the greatest player to ever play in a
Washington uniform. He was inducted into the Baseball Hall of Fame
in 1936. Ruicker Archive*

But Johnson played for lousy teams early on, and he didn't have a winning record until his fourth year in the big leagues. That season, 1910, he had a breakout year—a 25–17 record, 1.36 ERA, and a career-high 313 strikeouts. Johnson may have been a nice guy, but he knew his value. Holding out before the next season, he demanded that the team double his salary to $9,000. He finally settled on a three-year deal at $7,000 a year.

Despite having the game's best pitcher, the Senators continued to struggle. In his first five seasons, the Nationals finished in seventh place three times and last twice, including a 42–110 record in 1909—a .276 winning percentage. The team was so bad that year that in Johnson's five starts in July, Washington failed to score one run for him. It's no wonder that he lost a career-high 25 in 1909.

The franchise's fortunes changed dramatically in 1912, when Clark Griffith took over as manager. The Griffith name became synonymous with Washington baseball for the next half-century.

Griffith was born in a log cabin in Clear Creek, Missouri, in 1869. His father was shot and killed when Clark was just two years old, mistaken for a deer while hunting. Griffith later claimed that outlaw Jesse James had been a friend of his father's and slept in his home one night.

Young Clark and his siblings spent time growing up with relatives. "My early life made me very sympathetic toward orphans," he wrote years later. Griffith and his wife, known as "Aunt Addie," would adopt the children of her late brother, Jimmy Robertson, and the children would work for the team in one capacity or another, including Griffith's ultimate successor, Calvin.

That sympathy was manifested in other parts of his life as well. *Washington Post* sports editor Shirley Povich recalled years later being in Griffith's office one day when the newspaper ran photos of a widow and two small children on the sidewalk after being evicted.

"The tough little former pitcher who in one season had been thrown out of more baseball games than any other player in history, reacted to the eviction picture," Povich wrote.

Griffith told the team secretary: "Find these people and bring them to my house and rent them a house of their own before the day is over and pay the rent for six months and call some of our friends in Congress and get the lady a

Otis Clymer of Washington bats as John Kleinow of New York catches in this photo of a game from April 22, 1909. Library of Congress

job." Then he turned to Povich and said, "If this gets in the paper I'll take you out in the woodshed and give you what you deserve."

At seven, Griffith got his first taste of baseball as a mascot for a local team, and he became batboy two years later. After four years of semipro ball, he began his big league career with the St. Louis Browns of the American Association at the age of 21.

Griffith's build was all wrong for pitching. He was just five feet six inches tall, weighing 156 pounds, and the mustard on his fastball was definitely of the mild variety. Still, by cunning and grit—and no hesitation in scuffing up the ball—he became a very good pitcher, winning 20 games seven times and finishing his career with a .619 winning percentage and a 3.31 ERA. His best years were in the 1890s for Cap Anson's Chicago Colts.

But Griffith's true calling was not pitching, and in December 1900, he helped change the course of baseball. Ban Johnson, president of a minor circuit called the Western League, and Charles Comiskey, a Western League team owner, plotted along with Griffith to upgrade to big league status—the American League.

Griffith's main charge was to lure players away from the National League, giving the upstart organization instant credibility. Griffith, one of Comiskey's former players, prevailed upon 39 National Leaguers to switch leagues, according to a 1940 *Saturday Evening Post* profile.

When the league started up in 1901, Griffith became a player-manager of Comiskey's Chicago White Stockings, and led them to a first-place finish and the league's inaugural pennant. (The first World Series was still two years away.) Griffith also went 24–7 with a 2.66 ERA. In 1903, he became the first manager of the New York Highlanders. Griffith piloted the New York team for 5½ years, but quit in 1908 as the team was on its way to a last-place finish. Returning to his old league, he managed three years for the Cincinnati Reds, but was unhappy in the senior circuit. He would later refer to his time with the Reds as his "exile back in the National League."

Then a dream job opened up, although only in his eyes: managing in Washington. It wasn't exactly a plum gig, and many friends tried to talk Griffith out of taking a job in what was considered a baseball graveyard.

Washington had yet to have a winning record in 11 seasons, and was coming off its second straight seventh-place season entering the 1912 campaign. Griffith signed for $7,500 a year and paid $27,000 to buy a 10 percent ownership in the team, making him the single largest stockholder. He mortgaged his 6,000-acre Montana ranch for $20,000 to come up with most of the money.

Griffith immediately cleaned house. He traded catcher Gabby Street to New York, and unloaded several veteran players as part of a youth movement. On May 30, 1912, Griffith purchased 25-year-old first baseman Chick Gandil for $12,000. The Senators immediately reeled off 17 straight wins. Gandil would hit .305 that year, with 15 triples and 21 stolen bases in just 117 games.

Another 25-year-old player, Clyde Milan, became the team's spark plug. Milan, the outfielder who had been scouted along with Walter Johnson in 1907, batted .306 in 1912, with a league-best 88 stolen bases and 11 triples. Johnson, still just 24, went 33–12 with a 1.36 ERA and 303 strikeouts.

Under Griffith's guidance, the Senators catapulted up in the standings to second place. Not only did they have their first .500 season, but they played at nearly a .600 clip, finishing at .599. Griffith led the team to another second-place finish in 1913, when Johnson would have his best year ever—36–7, 1.14 ERA, 11 shutouts, and the first of his two Most Valuable Player awards. That season, Griffith offered the Detroit Tigers $100,000 for Ty Cobb, but was rebuffed. With Cobb and Johnson on the same team, there's no telling how good the Senators could have become.

But after the Senators slipped to a disappointing third place in 1914, they almost lost Johnson. In the off-season, the Big Train signed a contract with the Chicago team of the upstart Federal League. Griffith traveled to Kansas City to meet with Johnson, gave him a guilt trip about American League loyalty, and more importantly agreed to match the salary. Johnson remained a Senator.

Griffith would never win a pennant as manager of the Senators, but the "Old Fox" did lay the groundwork for the team's first pennant through smart trades and signings. In 1915, he landed outfielder Sam Rice for $600, and got first

The Senators in 1913. Library of Congress

baseman Joe Judge as a throw-in as part of another deal. Judge anchored Washington teams as an excellent defensive first baseman and perennial .300 hitter. Rice, a future Hall-of-Famer, hit .322 for his career.

As if an early proponent of Moneyball, Griffith continued to get young, cheap players who would pay dividends in the team's glory years of the 1920s. He bought second baseman Bucky Harris, who as a "boy wonder" manager led the team to its first pennant in 1924, for $4,000. He landed future Hall-of-Fame outfielder Goose Goslin, who blossomed into a .316 career hitter, for $6,000. Griffith also traded for shortstop Roger Peckinpaugh, who became the glue on Washington's steady infield. All of these players helped form the nucleus of the 1924 Senators team.

On the field, Griffith wasn't able to sustain the managerial magic of his first two seasons, when the team finished in second place. The next five years, Griffith-managed teams finished no better than third, and as low as seventh. After the 1919 season, Griffith found a wealthy backer, Philadelphia exporter William Richardson, and the two men bought a controlling interest in the team, with Griffith becoming team president.

He managed one season after that, but the team again finished in seventh place, and Griffith decided to replace himself as skipper with shortstop George McBride. Griffith changed managers each of the next three seasons after that, trying to find the winning formula. In 1924, he would finally find his man.

TWO

WASHINGTON'S ONLY CHAMPIONSHIP

TWO

WASHINGTON'S ONLY CHAMPIONSHIP

By 1923, all but two of the American League's eight teams had gone to the World Series at least once. The sad-sack St. Louis Browns and the Washington Senators were the only exceptions. Coming off two straight losing seasons and four managers in four years, the Nats gave no indication they would be pennant contenders in 1924. Owner Clark Griffith, who had been the first of those four managers, realized he needed to make a bold move, and offered the manager's job to his 27-year-old second baseman, Bucky Harris.

Griffith knew something about young managers. He had started his own skipper career at the age of 31, as player-manager of the Chicago White Sox in 1901, and led the team to an American League pennant that season. Still, sportswriters derided Harris's hiring as "Griffith's Folly."

"Those boys are going to get somewhere this year," Griffith insisted at the team's spring training facility in Tampa, Florida.

In fact, Washington had a pretty talented team, despite its mediocre record the previous couple of years. Its outfield featured two future Hall-of-Famers, Goose Goslin and Sam Rice, along with Nemo Leibold, all of whom hit .300 or better in 1923. Harris and fiery shortstop Roger Peckinpaugh provided a solid double-play combination, and first baseman Joe Judge provided outstanding defense and offense, batting .314 in 1923. Catcher Muddy Ruel hit .316, giving the team five .300 hitters. The only thing the offense lacked was power—no regular had hit more than nine home runs in 1923.

Walter Johnson, one of the greatest pitchers of all time, anchored a pitching staff that also included a pair of talented southpaws, George Mogridge and Tom Zachary, and a rubber-armed young reliever, Firpo Marberry. Johnson, 36, was not quite the unhittable pitcher he had been in his 20s and early 30s, when his ERA exceeded 2.00 only once in 10 seasons. Still, he was the ace of the staff, and his 1923 numbers were good by mortal standards—a 17–12 record and 3.48 ERA.

In the beginning, it looked like another typical Washington baseball season. After 28 games, the Senators were 12–16, the same record as the previous season, and the hiring of Harris as manager appeared to make no difference. Ty Cobb, the player-manager of the rival Detroit Tigers, made it tougher on the young manager by calling him "baby face" and "snookums."

Washington struggled to play .500 for the first two months of the year, and by mid-June, the Senators fell into sixth place with a 24–26 record. But the team won its next five games, providing some momentum heading into a four-game series against the first-place Yankees in New York.

The Nationals barged into Yankee Stadium by sweeping a Monday afternoon doubleheader, 5–3 and 4–2. They took the third game of the series the next day, 4–3, and completed the stunning four-game sweep by squeaking past the New Yorkers, 3-2. Looking up, the Senators found no one above them in the standings.

"Washington got hot quicker than almost any club I ever saw," Babe Ruth would write years later in his autobiography.

Eight thousand fans welcomed the team home upon its return to Union Station after the series. "Oh You Nationals!" the *Washington Post* declared. "Washington fans for the first time in their lives will experience the thrill of seeing the home representatives take the field tomorrow afternoon as the official defender of first place."

The Nationals extended their winning streak to 10 games the next day, as Johnson blanked the Athletics 5–0 in the first game of a doubleheader at Griffith Stadium. But the streak ended in the second game, when Ed Rommel shut out the Senators, 1–0.

By the time Washington and New York met again for a five-game series starting on July 4, the Nationals had opened up a four-game lead over their rivals. But the Yankees quickly stormed back into the race, taking four of the five games to pull within one game of the Senators.

Four days later, the Yankees reclaimed first place. They would hold on to it for most of July and August, while Washington kept close, never falling more than three games back. When the two teams met again in late August for another pivotal four-game series in New York—the teams' last matchup of the year—the Nationals had shaved the lead to ½ game.

In the opener, Babe Ruth smacked two home runs. But Goose Goslin hit for the cycle and the Nationals rallied for eight eighth-inning runs en route to an 11–6 victory, propelling the team into first place. The Senators took the second game, 5–1, but saw their pennant hopes flash before their eyes when a line drive off the bat of Wally Schang slammed into Walter Johnson's pitching hand.

The Big Train "crumpled up like an accordion," in the words of *Washington Post* sportswriter Frank H. Young. The game was delayed for five minutes as players from both teams gathered around Johnson, who was lifted from the game. Luckily for the Nats, the injury was not serious.

Although New York won the third game, 2–1, behind the pitching of Waite Hoyt, the Senators came back to take the series finale, 4–2, on a two-run double by Sam Rice in the top of the 10th inning, disappointing 45,000 fans in the Bronx. By winning three of the four games, Washington claimed the season series, 13–9. Even more impressive, the Nationals had won nine of eleven games played between the two teams at Yankee Stadium.

But the Yankees kept the pressure on their southern rivals. On September 1, Washington swept a doubleheader against the Philadelphia Athletics, but couldn't widen its lead, as the Yankees won both games of a twin-billing against the Red Sox. Two days later, New York pulled within one game, beating the Red Sox while the Nationals had the day off.

For the first two weeks of September, the two teams battled to a near-standstill in the standings, with New York gaining no more ground but Washington failing to pull more than two games ahead. The deadlock broke on September 15, when the Yankees finally caught the Nats by defeating the Chicago White Sox, 2–0, while Washington lost by an identical score to the Tigers in Detroit.

Not only did the Senators fall into a tie with New York, but they found themselves with only a four-game lead over third-place Detroit, the only other team still in the pennant race.

Washington's trip to Detroit kicked off a crucial four-city western road trip, which would also take the team to Cleveland, St. Louis, and Chicago. But the Senators did not face the usual road-field disadvantage. Fans across the country had taken to the Nats, the sentimental favorite that year, partly because the team had never won a pennant. More importantly, fans wanted to see Johnson finally make it to the World Series after all those years playing for lousy teams.

"There is more genuine interest in him than there is in a presidential election," Will Rogers wrote while the Yankees lost to the Tigers, 6–5, in Detroit. Sam Rice, Goose Goslin, and Earl McNeely paced Washington with four hits apiece. The Tigers, meanwhile, were reduced to playing spoiler; despite their victory, they had fallen seven games off the pace.

The prospect of the team's first pennant had Washington in a state of crazed excitement. Fans couldn't turn on ESPN for updates, but they could see the scores posted by the half-inning on walls of office buildings and groceries.

"Base ball in D.C. Classed Disease in Epidemic Form," declared a headline in the September 20 *Washington Evening Star*. The hyperbole continued in the story:

"Base ball in the National Capital no longer is a national game. It is a disease, a flaming epidemic, and if something doesn't happen soon to ease the strain on the faithful fans half the population of the District of Columbia will be dead of heart failure.

"No army fighting in foreign lands ever had the support that the old home town is giving to the Nationals in their dazzling fight for the American League pennant out there in the West, where men are men, where base hits are a blessing and errors the saddest words of tongue or pen."

Back then, the manly West referred to such rugged outposts as Cleveland, Detroit and Chicago. St. Louis constituted the baseball frontier, with no major league teams south or west of the city.

Even gray federal bureaucrats were getting swept up, the *Star* said: "In the Government departments Uncle Sam is losing thousands of dollars a day through the utter helplessness of his employees. They've got the base ball palsy."

If fans were truly on the verge of heart attacks, the Senators' next game would have sent them into cardiac arrest. A day after scoring 15 runs, Washington found that 14 just didn't cut it, losing to the Browns, 15–14, in 10 innings. Protecting a 14–13 lead with one out and the bases loaded in the bottom of the 10th, the Nationals had a chance to win when St. Louis pinch-hitter Herschel Bennett tapped one back to the mound for a potential double play.

But pitcher Firpo Marberry, rather than throw home to start a 1-2-3 twin-killing, turned around and threw the ball to second base. Unfortunately, no one was covering the bag, and the ball sailed into the outfield, allowing the tying and winning runs to score. Marberry's miscue was the team's sixth error of the game, and helped nullify three Washington comebacks. Starting pitcher Walter Johnson lasted just one inning, getting hammered for four runs.

"The Nationals made a terrible showing, especially for a team with pennant aspirations," the *Post* commented. The loss prevented the team from getting some breathing room from the Yankees, who also lost. The lead stayed at just one game.

"We were never so surprised in our lives at the way those western teams fought us—fought us in the face of the boos and protests of their own fans," Joe Judge recalled a few weeks later. "You know we knocked St. Louis out of the pennant race two years ago and I guess they just smacked their lips in anticipation when we landed in town, needing that series like we never needed anything else in our lives. Man, they came at us like an avalanche."

But Washington rebounded from the tough loss, winning the rubber game in St. Louis the next day while the Yankees again lost in Detroit, and widened the lead to two games.

That set the stage for the final seven games of the season. Washington would travel to Chicago for a three-game series against the White Sox and then finish the season at Fenway Park with a four-game set against the Red Sox—two of the league's bottom feeders. New York's schedule was nearly equally soft—three games on the road against Cleveland, followed by a four-game series in Philadelphia against the Athletics, also among the league's weaker teams.

But the seventh-place White Sox were not content to play out the string. "The Nationals now realize they have a hard fight on their hands," the *Star* reported after Washington won the first game, 8–3, behind Walter Johnson's 13th consecutive victory. The Sox ran the bases as if they, and not the Senators, were in a pennant race, "and when forced to slide did not hesitate to make the National infielders keep a sharp outlook for spikes."

Washington trailed for most of the game, but rallied for six runs in the seventh inning to turn a 3–1 deficit to a 7–3 lead. New York kept pace by beating the Indians, 10–4, in Cleveland.

The two American League pennant leaders continued to keep the heat on each other the next day. Washington eked out a 7–6 victory over the White Sox, nearly blowing a 7–3 lead, while New York beat Cleveland, 8–2. On September 24, the Nationals completed a three-game sweep of Chicago with a 6–3 victory, but the Yankees again stayed even, beating the Indians 2–0. Washington had finished its western tour by winning nine of twelve games.

"That the Yankees have been so persistent in their efforts to remain around the top of the heap has not bothered the Bucks greatly," the *Star* wrote, turning the Nats nickname into one named for the team's manager. "They have shaken off the Gotham horde three times this season and have no fear of it."

After a day off Thursday, both teams began their season-ending series on Friday. Washington immediately heightened tensions by losing to Boston, 2–1, while New York hammered the Philadelphia Athletics, 7–1. The loss snapped Washington's 4-game winning streak, Johnson's 13-game winning streak, and Sam Rice's 31-game hitting streak. Now Washington led by just one game with three to go.

In the loss to Boston, the Senators had a chance to tie the game in the ninth inning, but ran themselves out of a rally. With runners on first and third and two outs, Washington base runner Roger Peckinpaugh took off for second base on a delayed steal. But he was tagged out in a rundown before the runner on third, Ossie Bluege, could score.

A tie in the standings looked like a distinct possibility. In that case, New York and Washington would play a best-out-of-three playoff series to determine the pennant winner.

Manager Bucky Harris encouraged his depressed players to shake off the loss:

"We'll win our games and let those Yankees take care of themselves. Don't expect them to waver. Just see to it that we don't and we'll take the championship back to Washington Wednesday. We are good enough to win and if we play our game we will win."

The team responded with a 7–5 victory the next day that brought Washington tantalizingly close to its first pennant. Coupled with the Yankees' 4–3 loss in Philadelphia, Washington now had a two-game lead with just two games to go. The phrase "magic number" had not yet been coined, but people still grasped the concept. The Nats needed just one victory or one Yankees loss to clinch the pennant. Meanwhile over in the National League, the New York Giants had iced their fourth straight pennant by beating the Philadelphia Phillies, 5–1.

Both the Nationals and Yankees had to cool their heels the next day. Neither Boston nor Philadelphia played home games on Sundays back then because of Blue Laws. Trying to stay relaxed, Senators' players used the day off to sightsee around Boston, attend football games, or go fishing.

Although a Yankees loss would clinch a Nationals pennant, Manager Harris was not banking on it:

"We are going to put every ounce of fighting strength into tomorrow's game and pack away the old American League pennant; we are not depending on the Athletics beating the Yankees in Philadelphia either tomorrow or Tuesday, for I feel positive that we will experience little difficulty in disposing of the Red Sox in one of the remaining two games here, one victory assuring us of the first championship ever won by a Washington ball team."

Washington started Tom Zachary, the pitcher who had rescued the team in the previous game. But he didn't have it this time, surrendering two runs in three innings. Zachary did contribute offensively, going 2-for-2, and was lifted in the fourth inning for a pinch runner with Washington clinging to a 3–2 lead.

So once again the Nationals were forced to turn to their rubber-armed reliever, Firpo Marberry, although that rubber had been stretched thin of late. Marberry was making his 50th appearance of the season (including 14 starts), and his 10th in the team's last 19 games. Just the day before, he had complained of a sore arm, which was diagnosed as a slight muscle strain.

Marberry's arm had some elasticity left after all. He pitched five straight scoreless innings, giving up only three hits, and then started the ninth inning with a 4–2 lead. But with one out, pinch-hitter Danny Clark singled off Marberry, and Denny Williams, who had collected two hits on the day, came up with a chance to tie the game. But this time, he managed just a ground ball to second baseman Bucky Harris, and the player-manager stepped on second base and threw to first, for a pennant-clinching double play.

The celebration at Fenway Park that followed must have made the Senators feel like they had been playing on their home field. The 15,000 Red Sox fans were caught up in the national craze for the nation's capital team, with a little extra incentive—Washington's pennant denied Boston's hated rival, the Yankees, a chance to repeat as American League champions.

Hundreds of fans rushed onto the field to mob the Senators, and thousands more cheered the team as it left the field. They tossed straw hats into the air and waved handkerchiefs, and some lifted Nats owner Griffith from his seat in the stands and ferried him down to the dugout. Griffith, Harris, and Walter Johnson received standing ovations.

Meanwhile, back in Washington, in the days before fans could gather in sports bars to see their teams on the road, thousands had congregated in the drenching rain to watch the mechanical scoreboards register updates from Boston. More fortunate fans listened to the game indoors on the city's first radio station, WRC, which had just begun broadcasting two months earlier.

In Philadelphia, rain washed out the scheduled Yankees-Athletics doubleheader, and the meaningless games were not made up. New York's season was over. But having vanquished one New York team, Washington now had to take on another—the 10-time National League champion New York Giants. Washington's pennant broke up a Big Apple baseball monopoly—the previous three World Series had been New York-New York affairs.

"Naturally we are a happy lot, just like one big family, everybody tickled," Griffith said. "We are going after the World Series and realize in that connection that we are going up against the hardest club in the majors. The Giants have a wonderful ball club and are at their very best when the stakes are heaviest. I have no fear of the ball club cracking even though we are not as experienced as the Giants. We will give our best and it will be a series which Washington at least will long remember."

He added that the pennant "vindicated" his much-maligned decision to hire the young and unproven Harris as manager. "I knew he could do it and he did," Griff declared.

WASHINGTON BASE BALL CLUB

PENNANT WINNERS 1924

1924 winners of the American League Pennant. Library of Congress

For Harris, it was business as usual. Before leaving Boston to return to Washington, the player-manager told his players: "Winning the pennant means just another hard job for us, fellows, so after you land in Washington Wednesday get all the rest you can before reporting at the ball yard at 1 o'clock for practice."

The next day's *Star* ran a three-column cartoon featuring a smiling and celebrating Uncle Sam; the Washington Monument turned into semi-human form with outstretched arms, one hoisting a pennant; and even the Capitol Dome shaped like a baseball, with the bronze female statue on the top yelling, "Hooray!"

"The champions are not Washington's alone," wrote sportswriter John B. Keller. "They belong to the country, as typified in its National Capital, and the entire Nation insists upon sharing with Washington the joy and pride that follows the Griffmen."

President Calvin Coolidge, a Yankee in the literal sense (hailing from Vermont), sent a telegram to Manager Harris: "Heartiest congratulations to you and your team for your great work in bringing Washington its first pennant. We of Washington are proud of you and behind you. On to the world's championship."

Other branches of government celebrated as well. "The good news gives me a distinct thrill," said Supreme Court Justice William McKenna. "I am delighted and I am sure that all of Washington feels likewise."

The U.S. postmaster, James E. Power, traveled 3,000 miles from California—in the days before transcontinental flights—to attend the World Series. "Out in California, everybody was rooting for Washington to win," he said. Major league baseball on the West Coast was more than 30 years away.

Even Ty Cobb, the player-manager of the Detroit Tigers, jumped on the bandwagon. "I didn't win the pennant, but I had the consolation of kicking the Yankees out of the race and I got quite a kick out of that," he said, referring to Detroit's three-game sweep of New York in the final weeks of the season. He said he was rooting for Washington to win the series. "They are imbued with the competitive spirit and they'll fight hard."

On the train ride back to Washington, Judge said the team tapped the national affection for inspiration. "We knew that the country wanted us to win, and that's what helped to keep us fighting," he said. But Judge was miffed at a New York newspaper story that predicted easy pickings for the Giants. "This bird is going to be a lot wiser, but sadder, when this series is over," he said of the New York reporter.

If the Nationals needed some confidence, all they needed was a pep talk from their batboy, Frankie, who was practically blasé about the pennant.

The Senators comedy team of Al Schacht and Nick Altrock entertain fans during the 1924 World Series. Library of Congress

"What's all the fuss about?" the batboy told a newspaper reporter. "Goodnight, the time to shout was a month ago. Why, it was a cinch. We had that pennant all ironed out and properly creased with a special place built for it in my bat bag four weeks ago. The Giants? Say, you're not kidding me, are you? If you've got any extra money and want to make a lot more, easy, see, soak it all on the Nats. They're there, I tell you."

Frankie's bravado notwithstanding, the Giants posed a formidable challenge. The team had won its fourth straight pennant and featured future Hall-of-Fame manager John McGraw, already legendary in baseball circles. McGraw, one of the few managers to wear a suit and tie in the dugout rather than a uniform, had been at the helm of the Giants since 1902, guiding the team to 10 pennants.

Despite Walter Johnson, most observers gave New York the edge in pitching—then as now crucial in a short series. The Giants' rotation featured two 16-game winners, Virgil Barnes and Jack Bentley; talented lefthander Art Nehf, who went 14–4; and Hugh McQuillan, who posted a low 2.69 ERA. They performed especially strongly down the pennant stretch drive.

The offense featured an astonishing six future Hall-of-Famers: George Kelly, who led the league with 136 RBIs, and whose 21 homers were just one less than the entire Washington team; Frankie Frisch, the scrappy team captain and perennial .300 hitter; rookie Bill Terry, who later became the last .400 hitter in National League history; Travis Jackson, a .300 hitter and outstanding defensive shortstop; Ross Youngs, who led the team with a .356 batting average; and Hack Wilson, who six years later set the single-season RBI record.

Washington's offense stressed getting on base and manufacturing runs, with a special emphasis on the hit-and-run. Only one player hit more than three home runs—outfielder Goose Goslin, who finished with 12. In fact, the Senators' 22 homers during the regular season put them dead-last in the American League. But the lineup featured a trio of .300 hitters—Goslin (.344), Sam Rice (.334), and Joe Judge (.324)—and no regular batted below .268.

Aside from Johnson, Washington's pitching staff still had some solid "twirlers," as pitchers were often called back then. Southpaw George Mogridge won 16 games, and fellow lefty Tom Zachary won 15 with a 2.75 ERA. Curly Ogden, acquired during the season, rounded out the rotation with a 2.58 ERA. But there was concern that the staff had been spent by the end of the season. Some even expressed concern that Walter Johnson, despite his stellar season, had finished only 20 of his 38 starts. That would be considered a staggering success in modern-day baseball, but not by 1920s standards. The Big Train, who turned 37 at the end of the regular season, admitted he wasn't the same pitcher he had been in his prime.

Miss Elsie Tydings purchases the first ticket sold for a World Series in the nation's capital, 1924. Library of Congress

"I realize that I cannot go much further," he said. "My arm is still good, but I know I haven't got the stuff I used to have. When the season started I had fully made up my mind to retire at the end of this year. Now it all depends on what comes up this winter."

As usual, Johnson carried the capital's aspirations on his big shoulders. "I think we will win the World Series under any circumstances, but I am doubly sure we will win if Walter Johnson is right," Harris said.

Two thousand fans camped out at Union Station to greet the team upon its return to Washington Wednesday morning. In the afternoon, 100,000 people jammed Pennsylvania Avenue for a parade to celebrate the team's first pennant. The self-importance that marks Washington was dropped for a day, as the *Star* described it: "This debonair old capital of the United States completely forgot to take itself seriously in its eagerness to give its conquerors a welcome befitting champions."

Whistles, car horns, and cheers punctured the air along the procession, which included mounted policeman, a United States Cavalry Band, and red-coated members of the Washington Riding and Hunt Club. At the Ellipse by the White House, President Calvin Coolidge told the players: "By bringing the baseball pennant to Washington you have made the National Capital more truly the center of worthy and honorable national aspirations."

Coolidge, joined on the stage by Bucky Harris and Walter Johnson, presented the player-manager with a "loving cup" as a gift.

He also joked that now that the team had won the pennant, perhaps the city could actually get some work done. "When the entire population reached the point of requiring the game to be described play-by-play, I began to doubt whether the highest efficiency was being promoted," he said.

The president relayed that he received a telegram from Congressman John F. Miller of Washington State, asking that Coolidge call a special session of Congress that Saturday so that lawmakers could sneak out and go to the ballpark to see Walter Johnson pitch in the series opener.

"Mr. Miller has such judgment and his sense of public psychology is so accurate that I do not need to say what party he represents," Coolidge said of his fellow Republican.

After the president left, fans crowded around the stage and shouted out, "Three Cheers for Bucky!" . . . "Welcome Home Bucky!" . . . "Hello, Goose."

But soon word came of a scandal that threatened to derail the World Series. Commissioner Kenesaw Mountain Landis banned a player and coach on the National League champion Giants after learning of an alleged bribery plot. According to Philadelphia Phillies shortstop Heinie Sand, Giants outfielder Jimmy O'Connell had offered him $500 to throw a game against the Giants on the last weekend of the season. The Giants locked up the pennant with a victory in that very game. O'Connell then implicated one of his coaches, Cozy Dolan, as the mastermind behind the plan.

Coming only five years after the infamous Black Sox scandal, in which eight White Sox players had allegedly thrown the 1919 World Series, the sport's integrity was once again at stake. There was even a debate about whether the Fall Classic should be played at all. No less a figure than the American League president, Ban Johnson, second-guessed Commissioner Judge Kenesaw Mountain Landis's decision to go forward with it.

"In view of the public statements the World Series should have been called off," he said. Johnson also suggested there was probably a bigger plot to buy off Phillies players than had been revealed publicly. "It is my opinion that others of the Philadelphia players, in addition to Heine Sand, were approached in an effort to have games thrown," he said, calling for a federal investigation.

Pittsburgh Pirates owner Barney Dreyfuss joined Johnson in the criticism. "If this thing is not cleared up properly and to the entire satisfaction of the public by bringing every guilty man to justice—and there must be more than two involved—I will be in favor of eliminating the World Series, for a time at least, as a growing menace to the best interests of the game," he said. "It is absurd to say that O'Connell and Dolan were the only ones involved."

O'Connell, in fact, had fingered teammates Frankie Frisch, George Kelly, and Ross Youngs, but Landis cleared the three players. And the commissioner told Johnson and Dreyfuss to buzz off: "It seems to be time for those not clothed with responsibility to keep their shirts on," he said.

Ban Johnson telegraphed Griffith to tell him he would not attend the series, sending the Old Fox into a rage against his erstwhile ally. "Johnson is trying to play baseball politics, and is taking advantage of an unpleasant situation with which he has nothing to do, to put Judge Landis in a bad light," the Washington owner said. "We have waited years for this world's series and now Johnson wants to call it off, which would be manifestly unfair to the Senators and to the fans of this city, who have so loyally supported the team."

The series went forward, and it was another Johnson—Walter—who would be the focus of attention. Johnson was coming off an excellent regular season—23–7 with a 2.72 ERA, leading the American League in wins, winning percentage, ERA, strikeouts, and shutouts, and claiming the Most Valuable Player award. It was his best season since 1919. He even hit .283 with a .389 slugging percentage.

"Outside of the most rabid of Giant partisans, fans throughout this country will root for him in unison," predicted the Associated Press.

"All the sentiment of sentimental Washington is built around Johnson," *The New York Times* declared. "He is bigger than the Washington Monument, broader than the Potomac River." And the Nationals had the nation pulling for them, the *Times* observed: "Harris and his players are liked everywhere because they are young and dashing and enthusiastic. New York is hated because it has won too many pennants and possesses too much money and is too powerful."

Some things never change.

More than 150,000 fans tried to get tickets for the first two games at Griffith Stadium, which had been expanded to 36,000 seats to accommodate the World Series crowds. Prices ranged from a buck in the bleachers to six dollars for box seats. Some fans managed to gain admittance by securing jobs as peanut and soda vendors. Washington, still very much a southern city at the time, drew from points all across the South; there was not yet a team in Atlanta or Florida or even Texas. Downtown hotels were filled to capacity. Fans flooded in from the north too, as New Yorkers made the 200-mile trek down to catch their hometown Giants. An advertisement in *The New York Times* touted special World Series express trains to and from Washington.

But other New Yorkers made the trip to make a buck. Some set up "brokerage" offices to resell tickets at many times face value. Local police rounded up several of these scalpers, but were soon overruled by federal officials, who decided that brokers registered with the government could legally sell the tickets. Federal law, however, required the resellers to split their profits equally with the U.S. Treasury Department. Brokers who set up shop on "Scalpers Row" on Pennsylvania Avenue, just a few blocks from the White House, hawked tickets for as high as $100.

Meanwhile, thousands of fans lined up outside the ballpark with hopes of landing one of the last-minute bleacher seats, waiting all night for a shot at getting a ticket. Even here entrepreneurs plied their trade. "Place speculators" sold spots in line for fees of 50 cents to two dollars.

Hundreds of fans who couldn't get into the ballpark paid 50 cents each to watch the first game from the tops of wooden houses surrounding the ballpark. Another 12,000 gathered outside the *Washington Post* and *Evening Star* buildings to watch the game recreated on scoreboards.

New York City, always on the cutting edge, offered fans a chance to watch a reproduction of the game on a "Playograph," a scoreboard-type device that showed the position of the ball as it made its way around a baseball diamond, as well as the base runners.

At Griffith Stadium, the crowd included ordinary fans alongside Cabinet members, congressmen, senators, foreign ambassadors, and President Coolidge. "For once rank and title meant nothing in Washington," observed the *New York Times*.

An Army band warmed up the fans with *Sidewalks of New York* and *Dixie*. Although it was decades before million-dollar contracts, a couple of Washington Senators made out pretty well during the pre-game ceremonies. Washington fans, including the president, chipped in to buy Johnson an $8,000 Lincoln car, while shortstop Roger Peckinpaugh received a Peerless touring car from his hometown Cleveland fans. Coolidge threw out the first pitch, but his errant toss sent umpire Tom Connolly leaping for a one-handed grab.

The president's poor aim was a subtle reminder that he was not a huge fan of the game. That distinction belonged instead to his wife, Grace Goodhue Coolidge, who kept score and told him how the players were doing. The president listened, puffing on a cigar, sending smoke up that mingled with that of other fans' cigars and cigarettes, forming a hazy cloud in the ballpark. Men were decked out in suits, ties, and fedoras, while women wore dresses and fur-collared coats. On the field, Senators players leaned out of the dugout with their front feet on the playing field, and bats neatly laid out in front of them.

The pitching matchup featured the iconic Johnson, 37 years old, making his first World Series appearance, against the crafty 32-year-old southpaw Art Nehf, who had won the decisive games in the 1921 and 1922 World Series against the Yankees.

The Giants struck quickly. George Kelly hit a solo homer to left field off Johnson in the second inning, with the ball dropping into temporary bleachers that had been installed for the series. Bill Terry did the same in the fourth inning, and New York was up 2–0. Both balls may have been caught had the makeshift bleachers not been there.

Washington pulled within 2–1 in the sixth inning, when Earl McNeely doubled, moved to third on a grounder, and scored on an RBI groundout by Sam Rice. The Nationals went down in the seventh and eighth, however, and came to bat trailing by a run in the bottom of the ninth inning.

With one out, Ossie Bluege singled, and Peckinpaugh followed with a double off the left-field wall to tie the score, sending the crowd into a delirious uproar. The game had to be held up for several minutes as excited fans threw coats, hats, cushions, and newspapers on the field. A newspaper from the upper deck landed on Coolidge's hat, knocking it off-kilter, and the president took the advice of his Secret Service agents and sat down.

The Nationals stranded Peckinpaugh at second, and the game went into extra innings. In the 12th, Johnson struck Hank Gowdy in the ribs, putting the potential go-ahead run on first. Next was Nehf, who lifted a fly to center field. McNeely charged and tried to make a shoestring catch, but the ball squirted free. Worse, he fired wildly past second baseman Harris, and now the Giants had runners on second and third with nobody out.

McGraw, having already left his pitcher in to bat earlier in the inning, now sent a second pitcher to the plate, Jack Bentley, to pinch-hit. But Bentley, a former National, wasn't your typical weak-hitting hurler. In two seasons with New York, he had hit .342. Washington intentionally walked him to load the bases.

The next batter, Frisch, hit a ground ball to second, and Harris forced Gowdy at the plate. But Young followed with a soft single to center field, giving the Giants a 3–2 lead. Kelly followed with a sacrifice fly to left to make it 4–2.

The Senators scratched back in their half of the inning. Mule Shirley, pinch-hitting for Johnson, reached second base when shortstop Travis Jackson dropped a pop-up. One out later, Harris singled Jackson home to bring the Nationals within one. Rice followed with another single, sending the potential tying run to third, but tried to stretch the hit into a double and was thrown out. Now Washington had a runner on third with two outs, instead of first-and-third with one out.

The game came down to a race between an infield throw to first and a sprint from third base to home. Back then, a runner could score on the third out if he crossed home plate before the out was made. Goslin hit a slow grounder to second, and the Giants' second baseman, Kelly, whipped the ball to first a fraction of a second before Harris stepped on home plate, in the eyes of umpire Bill Klem.

The Senators erupted at Klem, according to a book on the 1924 season by Joe Judge's grandson, Mark Gauvreau Judge. Goslin, Harris, Judge, and Nick Altrock surrounded the umpire.

"The other players backed off, but Judge kept arguing, following the umpire off the field," Judge wrote. "They were just ahead of Calvin Coolidge, and when the president passed by Judge and Klem, the bickering pair didn't even notice."

The loss was especially disappointing to Johnson. Some longtime Johnson-watchers said he seemed nervous and tried too hard. "Walter yesterday worked with a degree of deliberation that caused widespread comment," the *Star* observed. "He seemed from the very outset to be debating with himself at great length over every delivery he made."

In 12 innings, Johnson had thrown 165 pitches, surrendering two homers and a whopping 14 hits, but also striking out 12 batters.

"Walter pitched a great game," said Nehf, who had out-pitched the legend. "It was mighty fine to win, of course, but it would not have been hard to lose to the man I opposed today. There were moments when victory hung on a thread."

McGraw, in a syndicated column, called it the "greatest World Series game ever played. . . . In all my experience, I never have seen a game harder played."

The next day, Washington sent Tom Zachary to the mound against Bentley, the former Senator. Washington jumped out to an early 2–0 lead, thanks to a two-run homer by Goose Goslin. Bucky Harris made it 3–0 with a solo homer into the temporary bleachers in the fifth. The Giants plated a run in the seventh, and entered the ninth trailing 3–1.

But Zachary, who had held New York to just four hits through the first eight innings, began to falter. He walked the leadoff batter, Frisch, on four pitches. One out later, Kelly singled to right field, and Frisch scored all the way from first base after right fielder Rice bobbled the ball. Kelly moved into scoring position on a groundout, and now Washington needed only one more out to even the series.

But Hack Wilson deflated the fans with an RBI single to right field, bringing Kelly home with the tying run. Zachary was done, and Marberry came in to extinguish the rally by striking out Travis Jackson.

Now in danger of falling behind two games to none, the Nationals knew they had to pull this one out. In the bottom of the ninth, Judge worked a leadoff walk and moved to second on a sacrifice. The crowd cheered wildly as Peckinpaugh came to the plate. The Washington shortstop had made the most of his RBI opportunities during the regular season, driving in 73 runs while hitting only two homers. Now he ripped a line drive down the left-field line for a hit, and Judge crossed the plate with the winning run. But Peckinpaugh pulled a tendon in his leg while sprinting to first base, which would cost him playing time in the series.

Back then, there were no off days in the World Series, so the two teams squared off the next day at the Polo Grounds, located in upper Manhattan. Games three, four, and five would be played there, while game six, if necessary, would be played back in Washington. A coin toss would determine the location of a possible seventh game.

Even in the World Series, the Nationals maintained their road-fan appeal, as many New York fans cheered on the visitors. Some Giants fans even taunted their own team's role in the bribery scandal, shouting, "Where's Jimmy O'Connell?" and "Put Cozy Dolan on the coaching line!"

In Washington, meanwhile, some fans who weren't satisfied looking at mechanical scoreboards or listening on the radio watched the U.S. Marines pantomime the game at Griffith Stadium.

Peckinpaugh tried to play through his injury, but lasted only into the third inning, forcing Washington to adopt a makeshift defense on the left side of the infield. Third baseman Ossie Bluege moved to shortstop, and Ralph Miller took over at third base. Peckinpaugh's injury proved costly, as Miller made an error in the sixth inning that led to an unearned run.

Washington started Marberry, normally a relief pitcher, but he fell behind 3–0 and didn't make it out of the fourth inning. By the top of the ninth, the Nationals trailed 6–3. Washington loaded the bases and pulled within two runs on a one-out walk to Bluege, but could get no closer. The Giants held on for a 6–4 victory, and a 2–1 series lead.

The Nationals got better luck from their starting pitcher in the next game, as George Mogridge went seven-plus innings, allowing only two runs on three hits. He left the game to an enthusiastic ovation from the New York not-so-faithful. Goose Goslin fueled the Washington offense, going 4-for-4 with a home run and four RBIs, to pace the Senators' 7–4 victory.

"For the country at large the eagle may remain the national bird, but for the National Capital the greatest bird that flies is the goose," the *Post* opined.

Goslin, it turned out, had received some pretty good hitting advice before the game. "Babe Ruth came to me before the game and told me I was swinging wrong," Goose said. "So I started swinging another way, and you could see the result yourself. I sure do owe a lot to the Babe."

Ruth was among several celebrity athletes at the game. Yankees Joe Dugan and Whitey Witt were also there, along with former Giant player and future Yankees manager Casey Stengel, Ty Cobb, Christy Mathewson, Rogers Hornsby, George Sisler, and boxer Jack Dempsey.

"Goose" Goslin, Washington's fabled power hitter, who was inducted into the Baseball Hall of Fame in 1968. Rucker Archive

Washington was confident it could take command of the series. It sent Johnson to the mound for the pivotal game five. A win by the ace would send the series back to Washington with the Nats up three games to two. But once again, Johnson didn't have his good stuff. The Giants hammered him for 13 hits and six runs in eight innings, including four hits by 18-year-old Freddy Lindstrom. A Washington castoff, Bentley, out-pitched the greatest pitcher of the era, and even smacked two hits off him, including a two-run homer in the fifth inning, giving the Giants a lead they would never relinquish.

Johnson's grandson, Henry W. Thomas, recounted an incident that demonstrated the depth of the pitcher's fan appeal. As the Big Train was getting pounded, the stunned crowd was mostly silent, but one fan started yelling, "Take him out! Take him out!" Sitting in the same section of the stadium was umpire Billy Evans, a longtime friend of Johnson's.

"Appalled fans around the man were already turning on him in outrage as Evans came charging over, yelling, 'Let him alone, let me have him. He's mine,'" Thomas wrote in a biography of his grandfather. Only the intervention of fans prevented a fistfight.

The game was close for 7½ innings. Trailing 3–1, Washington pulled within 3–2 on an eighth-inning solo home run by Goslin. But the Giants broke the game open in the bottom of the frame, scoring three runs off Johnson. The zip on Johnson's fastball had faded, and he made matters worse by making a key error.

Johnson said after the game he would likely retire. With no more starts scheduled in the series, it appeared as if the Big Train had sputtered on his final ride. Scribes from both cities bemoaned such an unfitting end to such a glorious career. The *Times* led its story the next day like an obituary:

"Giant bats penned one of the saddest stories ever known to baseball yesterday. After the name of Walter Johnson they wrote 'finis,' for it was Johnson, before the second greatest crowd of the series, who tried again and failed again. When Johnson's own world's series finally came along he couldn't win a single game. . . . Even for 52,000 New Yorkers it was a tragic affair and Johnson the most tragic figure that ever stalked through a world's series."

The *Post* had a nearly identical take: "No sadder scene was ever presented in World Series annals than the one that was played before 50,000 spectators today."

In the clubhouse after the game, Johnson read telegraphs that had come in during the game wishing him success. "I couldn't hold the Giants, I just couldn't hold them," he said. "These telegrams make me feel worse about it than ever. I've received wires from all over the world telling me how everyone was pulling for me to win, and I couldn't come through for them. I wish I could have. It's not very encouraging to know that I'll finish up my career in the big leagues with two World Series defeats, but I don't think I'll come back next year."

Harris at least brought some good news to the team's clubhouse. He had won a coin toss, meaning if Washington could win game six at home, game seven would be played there as well. "We'll get them in the seventh game," the Washington skipper declared. "This series isn't lost yet by any matter or means."

Peckinpaugh, the fiery shortstop whose injury had kept him out of most of game three and all of games four and five, vowed to play again. The team sorely missed his steady defense. "I'll be in there if I have to tear the leg off and throw it away when the game is over," he said. "My leg doesn't feel any too well, but I'll play if I have to stand on one foot."

Facing elimination the next day, Washington fell behind quickly when New York's George Kelly hit an RBI single off Tom Zachary in the first inning. The Washington pitcher settled down after that, but the Nats couldn't get anything going off the Giants' Nehf, who had also handcuffed them in the series opener. When the Senators came to bat in the bottom of the fifth inning, they trailed 1–0.

Peckinpaugh limped to the plate to lead off, and lined a base hit down the left-field line. Muddy Ruel sacrificed him to second, and Zachary's groundout advanced him to third with two outs. McNeely walked and stole second. Then Harris got an outside pitch and went with it, driving a single to right field, scoring both runs and giving Washington a 2–1 lead.

In the top of the ninth inning, Peckinpaugh's vow to play on one foot if necessary was tested. The Giants got the tying run on base with one out, and Irish Meusel bounced a ball up the middle. Ranging to his left, the limping Peckinpaugh raced over to the ball, fielded it, and tossed it to second base for a force play. He immediately went down after landing awkwardly on his bad leg, and had to be carried off the field. Peck was finally done for the series. Zachary sealed the victory by striking out Hack Wilson.

Peckinpaugh's double-play partner and manager, Harris, saluted him in a column the next day. "His statement the day previous that he'd play ball yesterday if he had to break his leg was almost borne out," Harris wrote. "He didn't break his leg, but he turned a tendon, opened up an old charley horse and must have suffered the agonies of the damned. If that isn't gameness, there's no such thing in athletics."

On a Sunday afternoon in Washington, the two teams squared off for the seventh game—the first time a series had gone the distance in twelve years. New York started Virgil Barnes, who had surrendered five runs in five innings as the starter in game four. Washington gave Curly Ogden his first start of the series, but it was actually a ruse by Harris to get Bill Terry, the rookie Giants left-hander hitter, out of the game.

Terry had obliterated the Washington pitching staff for a .500 batting average through the first six games, but he didn't hit left-handed pitchers well and McGraw often sat him against southpaws. Harris decided to start the right-handed pitcher Ogden, then bring in a left-handed pitcher, Mogridge, in the first inning, forcing McGraw to make a choice: either leave Terry in to face a left-handed pitcher, or take him out and have him unavailable for the reminder of the game.

Ogden, making his only World Series appearance, faced just two batters, striking out one and walking the other, before Harris made the switch to Mogridge. McGraw decided to leave Terry in the game, at least for a while. Harris's gambit worked—the red-hot Terry went 0-for-2 before being lifted for a pinch-hitter in the sixth inning. Harris also enjoyed success as a hitter, smoking one into the temporary bleachers in left field to give Washington a 1–0 lead in the fourth inning. It was Harris's second homer of the series, after hitting just one the entire regular season.

But New York came storming back in the sixth. After putting men on first and third with nobody out, the Giants sent right-handed hitter Irish Meusel in as a pinch-hitter for Terry. Harris countered with right-handed reliever Marberry, and Johnson began warming up in the bullpen. Meusel greeted Marberry's first pitch for a sacrifice fly to right field, tying the game.

Then Washington's defense became unglued at the worst possible time. After a single by Hack Wilson put runners at first and second, Travis Jackson hit a ground ball to Judge at first base. But Judge fumbled the ball for an error, allowing the go-ahead run to score. The next batter, Hank Gowdy, hit a ground ball to shortstop, and it looked like Washington would get out of the inning with a 6-4-3 double-play. But the ball went through the legs of Ossie Bluege, normally a third baseman who was filling in for the injured Peckinpaugh. Now the Giants were up 3–1.

Washington went down in order in the sixth inning, and managed two hits in the seventh, but could not score. With one out in the bottom of the eighth, pinch hitter Nemo Leibold doubled down the left-field line. He moved to third base on a Muddy Ruel's first hit of the series. Backup catcher Bennie Tate, pinch-hitting for Marberry, walked on a 3–2 pitch to load the bases.

With one out and the top of the order coming up, Washington would have two shots at tying the game on a base hit. McNeely flied out to left, and the runners stayed put. Up came Harris, whose homer had accounted for all of Washington's offense up to that point. The player-manager smacked a groundball to third that proved to many that the Senators were a team of destiny—or at least a team with a friendly home infield. The ball took a bad hop over third baseman Freddy Lindstrom's head and sailed into left field, tying the score at 3–3.

The game was stopped for several minutes as Griffith Stadium convulsed in celebration. Confetti, thousands of pieces of ripped-up newspapers, hats, and coats were thrown onto the field. Wild cheers were mixed in with the sounds of whistles, bells, and horns. McGraw then sent in Nehf, who got Rice to ground out to end the threat.

The fans continued to cheer as the Nationals took the field in the top of the ninth inning, because coming in to pitch one last time was Walter Johnson. He had a chance for redemption that no one could have predicted after his game-five loss, but equally possible was that he'd lose again—and finish the series with an 0-and-3 record. And after getting the first batter out, Johnson came dangerously close to losing his third World Series game, as Frisch tripled to deep center field.

Washington intentionally walked the next batter, Ross Youngs, who had hit .356 during the regular season. But there was no relief in the Giants lineup, as NL RBI leader George Kelly came to the plate. In the previous matchup in game five, Kelly had singled off Johnson to start the eighth-inning rally that put the game out of reach. But this was not the same tired Johnson of just two days ago. The Big Train threw fastballs by Kelly for a crucial strikeout. He then induced Meusel to ground out to third.

In the bottom of the inning, Washington also got a man to third base with one out when Judge singled to center and advanced to third on an infield error. But Ralph Miller, who had replaced Tommy Taylor at third base, grounded into a rally-killing double-play. So game seven would end just as the opening game had—in extra innings.

Johnson gave up a leadoff walk to start the 10th inning, but a strikeout and double-play quickly extinguished the threat. The Senators went down in order in the bottom of the inning, as Harris let Johnson bat rather than lift him for a pinch-hitter.

In the 11th, the Giants again had Johnson on the ropes. With a runner on second and one out, Johnson faced Frisch, who had tripled off him just two innings earlier. This time, Johnson struck out the Giants' captain, and then, for the second straight time, intentionally walked Ross Youngs and struck out George Kelly, ending the rally. In Washington's half of the inning, Goslin doubled with one out, but was stranded there.

Johnson had his good stuff, but he continued to make the game stressful for the hometown fans. Meusel led off the 12th inning with a single, the third straight inning the Giants got the leadoff man on against the Washington pitcher. But Johnson struck out Hack Wilson, and retired the next two batters on a force out and fly ball. Johnson had pitched his fourth inning of relief, just two days after pitching eight innings.

With one out in the bottom of the inning, Ruel popped a foul behind home plate, and it looked like the Senators would go quietly. But catcher Hank Gowdy tripped over his own mask, which he had thrown to the ground to get a view of the ball, and Ruel had another shot. He took advantage, lining a double past third base. Harris again let Johnson bat for himself, and he reached first on an error by shortstop Travis Jackson. Ruel stayed put at second base.

Washington had had good luck with the area around third base back in the eighth inning, when Harris's bad-hop single tied the game. Why not take a shot at the same neighborhood? McNeely did just that, grounding a ball to third, and incredibly, the ball took another bad bounce and skipped over third baseman Lindstrom's head. Ruel chugged home with the winning run at 5:04 p.m. without drawing a throw.

Fans jumped out onto the field and danced on the tops of the dugouts, while police came to rescue players from the masses. The fans surrounded McNeely before he even reached first base on his series-winning hit, and his shirt was torn by the time he got to the dugout. "He was thumped and pummeled and hugged and reached the bench a very crushed young man," the *New York Times* wrote.

McNeely was dubbed the "$50,000 man," because the team had paid that princely sum to purchase him in August.

Legendary sportswriter Frederick G. Lieb, who was the official scorer of the World Series, wrote: "Perhaps the millions of fans pulling for Washington to win its first World Series championship influenced the usually fickle goddess of luck to give a little lift to the gallant Nationals."

Meanwhile in the clubhouse, Johnson told a reporter: "I'm the happiest man in the world—the happiest man in the world. Tell everybody I'm tickled to death and anything else along the same line you can think of. I'll stand back of

The 1924 World Champion Washington Senators with President Calvin Coolidge (standing center-left, black arm band on left sleeve) at the White House. Rucker archive

anything you say, as I can't express my feelings in words at all right now. I can never thank Bucky enough for having confidence in me again after my two other failures, and I'm happy I didn't disappoint him and my friends."

Harris said he believed in his aging ace all along. "Walter was my best bet," he said. "That's why I put him in. Anyone who thought Walter was through was a fool. I knew he was all right." Harris said he also had visions of the game ending in a tie, because "I knew absolutely that they couldn't score on Walter if we played all night, and we didn't seem to be able to get the breaks."

The Giants' losing pitcher, Jack Bentley, suggested there may have been a higher power at work. "The good Lord just couldn't bear to see a fine fellow like Walter Johnson lose again," he said.

New York World sportswriter Heywood Broun waxed more poetically: "I was never swept by the Easter story until I saw the seventh game of the World's Series. I have seen Osiris die in the darkness and come back from his cavern into the sunlight to conquer. Mithra, Adonis, Krishna, Atlas, Hercules—all these I take to be symbols of the human spirit, and so without incongruity I may add Walter Johnson to the list."

Fans celebrated well past midnight, honking horns, blasting sirens, blowing whistles, and shaking rattles. Cars on Pennsylvania Avenue were forced to drive on streetcar tracks as thousands of fans jammed the street. People threw torn-up newspapers from office buildings.

"In spontaneity and unadulterated enthusiasm the demonstration yesterday afternoon and last night exceeded any-thing of its kind in the history of Washington," the *Post* reported. "It was an Armistice Day and Mardi Gras blended into one. It was the thrilling outburst of a city's joy which knew no bounds. It was wonderful."

Giants' Manager John McGraw called it the best World Series ever played. "There were more thrills to the square inch in these seven games than any baseball man ever saw," he wrote in a syndicated column. In a follow-up column, he conceded that Washington winning the series was the "greatest thing that could have happened to baseball. It was a popular victory."

THREE

GLORY YEARS

THREE

GLORY YEARS

Washington's 1924 World Series championship ushered in the franchise's only true golden age. In a decade covering the Roaring '20s and the early years of the Great Depression, the team won three pennants, along with a second-place finish and three third-place finishes. Only once did the Senators fail to finish in the top half of the eight-team league, which was known as the "first division" in those days before divisional play.

Senators owner Clark Griffith did not coast on the success of the '24 team. He went out and upgraded the starting pitching rotation with two brilliant moves in the off-season. First, he acquired 35-year-old veteran right-hander Stan Coveleski from the Cleveland Indians in exchange for two inconsequential players. Coveleski, a cagey spitballer and future Hall-of-Famer, eclipsed Walter Johnson as the ace of the pitching staff in 1925, going 20–5 for a league-high .800 winning percentage, and also posting a league-best 2.84 ERA.

In another steal, Griffith purchased Dutch Ruether from Brooklyn, and the southpaw went 18–7 for the Senators in 1925. Meanwhile, the 37-year-old Johnson may not have been the staff ace, but he posted a 20–7 record and a 3.07 ERA. He also hit an astonishing .433.

Several everyday players had great seasons too. First baseman Joe Judge batted .314, catcher Muddy Ruel hit .310, outfielder Sam Rice stroked a team-best .350 with 87 RBIs, and outfielder Goose Goslin hit .334 with 18 home runs and 113 RBIs. He also led the league with 20 triples. No regular hit lower than .286.

Backed by great starting pitching and a deep lineup, the Senators cruised to the American League pennant in 1925. This time, the Yankees weren't even in sight, finishing in seventh place, 28½ games behind the Senators. New York had to play the first two months without Babe Ruth, who was sidelined with an ulcer. Finishing with a .636 winning percentage, the Senators won the pennant by a comfortable 8½ games over the Philadelphia Athletics. The Senators also set a franchise record by drawing 817,000 fans, shattering the mark the team had set the year before, when it drew 584,000.

This time, the Senators matched up against the underdog Pittsburgh Pirates in the World Series, but Pittsburgh had a dangerous lineup. The Bucs led the National League in hitting with a .307 batting average, and also paced the league in doubles, triples, on-base percentage, slugging percentage, and of course, runs. Only one regular, second baseman Eddie Moore, batted lower than .300, and that was just barely—.298. Four Pirates drove in at least 100 runs.

Pitcher Stan Coveleski in 1925. Library of Congress

The lineup featured three future Hall-of-Famers—shortstop Kiki Cuyler, who led the team with a .357 batting average; third baseman Pie Traynor, who hit .320; and outfielder Max Carey, who hit .343 and led the league with 46 stolen bases.

It was to be a mirror image of the 1924 series for Walter Johnson. The Big Train, who had lost his first two starts in the '24 series, won his first two starts against the Pirates, staking the Senators out to a commanding 3–1 series lead. But his victory in the fourth game came at a cost. In the third inning, Johnson singled to left and strained his leg while trying to stretch the hit into a double.

His teammates couldn't hold the series lead. Coveleski, the Nats' most dependable pitcher in the regular season, lost game five at Griffith Stadium, 6–3, his second World Series loss. The Senators wasted a solid performance by Alex Ferguson in game six at Forbes Field, dropping the game, 3–2.

So again Washington's season would come down to one game. The Senators turned to—who else?—Johnson to start game seven. The conditions in Pittsburgh were not good for a pitcher getting over a leg injury. The game had to be postponed once because of rain, and when the two teams squared off on another cold, rainy day the next afternoon in Pittsburgh, the field was wet and muddy.

The next day's *New York Times* described the game as "the wettest, weirdest and wildest game that fifty years of baseball has ever seen. . . . Water, mud, fog, mist, sawdust, fumbles, wild throws, wild pitches, one near fistfight, impossible rallies—these were mixed up to make the best and the worst game of baseball ever played in this century. Players wallowing ankle-deep in mud, pitchers slipping as they delivered the ball to the plate, athletes skidding and sloshing, falling full length, dropping soaked baseballs—there you have part of the picture that was unveiled on Forbes Field this dripping afternoon. It was a great day for water polo."

The Senators jumped out to a 4–0 lead in the first inning, but the Bucs rallied for three runs in the third. Washington outfielder Joe Harris doubled in two runs in the fourth to give the Nationals a 6–3 lead. That should have iced the game with the durable Johnson on the mound, who had already pitched two complete games. But the Big Train was pitching on a slippery track, and could not put the game away.

After pulling within 6–4 in the fifth inning, the Pirates tied the score with two runs in the bottom of the seventh. The rally started with an error by shortstop Roger Peckinpaugh, incredibly the seventh of the series for the normally reliable infielder. Peckinpaugh, who had hit only four home runs in the regular season, made amends for the miscue by

The Republican baseball team of the House of Representatives at American League Park on May 3, 1926.

slamming a homer into the left-field seats in the top of the eighth, giving Washington a 7–6 lead. But Peckinpaugh made yet another error in the bottom of the inning, and the Pirates scored three runs to take a 9–7 lead. Pittsburgh held on to win the game, becoming the first team in history to come back from a 3–1 World Series deficit.

For both Peckinpaugh and Johnson, the series marked a reversal of fortune. Peck had played such a heroic 1924 World Series, overcoming injuries to make clutch plays that helped Washington win its first championship. Now he was a goat. Johnson, who atoned for two losses in the '24 World Series by winning a dramatic game seven, now lost a game seven after winning his first two games. In the deciding game, Johnson was pounded for 15 hits and nine runs, although only five runs were earned.

American League President Ban Johnson second-guessed manager Bucky Harris's use of Johnson for three games. "You sacrificed a World's Championship for our league through your display of mawkish sentiment," he lectured the young manager in a telegraph. But Johnson's final line was still good: a 2–1 record, a 2.08 ERA. And Harris replied testily: "You run the American League and I'll manage the Washington baseball team."

The next year, Washington slipped to fourth place. The bats were still there—six of the eight regulars hit .290 or better, including Buddy Myer, who replaced the aging Peckinpaugh at shortstop and batted .304. Goslin had another monster year, hitting .354 with 17 home runs and 108 RBIs. But the pitching dropped off considerably.

Walter Johnson started things off brilliantly, winning a 1–0, 15-inning pitching duel over the Philadelphia Athletics's Eddie Rommel on opening day, fanning 12 batters. But Johnson, now 38 years old, would have his worst season since breaking into the major leagues 20 years earlier. He finished with a 15–16 record and a 3.63 ERA, and would pitch only one more season.

Coveleski turned in another good year in 1926, winning 14 games with a 3.12 ERA, but he was not the dominating pitcher he had been the year before. The rest of the rotation was subpar. The Senators still finished with a decent winning percentage of .540, but the Yankees were back at the top of the league. Babe Ruth returned to form, batting .372 with 47 home runs and 146 RBIs. And a young first baseman named Lou Gehrig chipped in 16 homers and 112 RBIs.

Washington improved slightly in 1927, finishing in third place with a .552 percentage, but nobody could compete with the Yankees that year. New York put together its infamous "Murderer's Row," with Ruth setting a single-season record with 60 home runs—more than any other team in the league—and Gehrig batting .373 with 47 home runs and 175 RBIs. New York won 110 games and finished 25 games ahead of the Nationals.

Meanwhile, a line drive off the bat of Joe Judge in spring training broke Johnson's leg. He pitched only 100 innings that season, going 5–6 with a 5.10 ERA, and decided to retire after the season.

"The fact that he didn't seem to weigh heavily in the team's pitching scheme ultimately decided the issue," wrote Johnson's grandson, Henry W. Thomas, in his biography, *Walter Johnson: Baseball's Big Train.* "Despite a great deal of speculation in the press as to the veteran's plans, there had been no communication from Griffith, and Johnson took it as a sign that perhaps he was no longer wanted." Griffith insisted later that was not the case.

With Johnson done, Griffith admirably patched up the Senators' starting rotation in 1928. He acquired pitchers Sad Sam Jones and Milt Gaston from the St. Louis Browns for outfielder Earl McNeely and pitcher Dick Coffman. Jones would turn in a great season, going 17–7 with a 2.84 ERA.

A trade that Griffith had made in 1926 also paid dividends for the 1928 team. The Old Fox had traded Dutch Ruether to the New York Yankees for Garland Braxton. Ruether was out of baseball by 1928, while Braxton led the American League with a 2.51 ERA that year. At the plate, the Senators got another terrific season from Goslin, who led the league with a .379 batting average, the first time a Senator had won the batting crown since Ed Delahanty's .376 in 1902.

Despite the individual accomplishments, the team slumped to fourth place with a 75–79 record, its first sub-.500 season in five years. It was also the first time player-manager Bucky Harris failed to guide the team to a winning record. His playing tanked as well; Harris hit just .204. The home crowd turned on Harris, yelling, "Take him out!"

Griffith did just that after the season, firing the only manager to take the Senators to the World Series. Speculation on a successor focused around first baseman Joe Judge and catcher Muddy Ruel, but two weeks later Griffith decided to go for an even bigger name—Walter Johnson.

Some baseball writers wondered if the kind-hearted Johnson might be too soft for the job. At his signing, Johnson said he would "go to the whip" when necessary, adding he would not tolerate loafing. "Washington players at least will be expected to give their all, and if they don't there is no room for them on the team," he said.

Nearly 41, Johnson even held out the possibility of pitching again for the team. "I really believe that I still have a few good games in my arm," he said, but he never pitched again. For Griffith, hiring a Senators player as skipper continued a precedent he had set when he made shortstop George McBride manager in 1921. All five of Griffith's managers, including Johnson, had played for the Senators.

Meanwhile, Harris quickly landed the manager's job with the Detroit Tigers. Although only 32 when the season started, Harris was effectively done playing—he appeared in only seven games in his first year as Detroit skipper that season and four more the rest of his career. Harris now focused exclusively on managing, returning later for two more tours of duty with the Senators.

At first, Johnson had little success as manager. In 1929, the team finished in fifth place with a .467 winning percentage, 34 games out of first place, and two games ahead of Bucky Harris's Tigers. Goslin dropped nearly 100 points from his batting title year, to .288. Sam Jones slumped to 9–9 with a 3.92 ERA. The Senators drew just 355,000 fans, their worst attendance since 1919.

But Johnson turned things around the next year, and Washington zoomed to second place in 1930, finishing with a .610 winning percentage. That record would be good enough to win the pennant most seasons, but not this year. The Senators finished eight games behind the Philadelphia Athletics, a dynasty-in-the-making packed with future Hall-of-Famers like Jimmy Foxx, Al Simmons, Mickey Cochrane, and Lefty Grove. Still, 1930 proved to be a success for the Senators both on the field and at the gate. The team drew 614,000 fans, nearly double the year before—even though it was the first season played in the Great Depression.

In a year dominated by offense, the Nats had a league-best 3.96 ERA and 78 complete games. Five pitchers won at least 15 games under Johnson's tutelage—Bump Hadley, Alvin Crowder, Lloyd Brown, Fred Marberry, and Sam Jones. All but one had exactly 15 wins, with Lloyd Brown leading the staff with 16 victories. Baseball went nearly 70 years before another team featured five 15-game winners—the 1998 Atlanta Braves pitching staff of Denny Neagle, Tom Glavine, Greg Maddux, John Smoltz, and Kevin Milwood.

At the plate, six Washington regulars hit .300 or better, led by outfielders Heinie Manush (.362) and Sam Rice (.349) and shortstop Joe Cronin, who hit .346 with 13 home runs and 126 RBIs and won the *Sporting News* American League Player of the Year award. Manush and Cronin were two recent acquisitions Griffith made as he built up Washington's last great team.

The Senators acquired Manush in a midseason exchange of top-flight hitters with the St. Louis Browns, in which Washington parted reluctantly with Goose Goslin. Two years earlier, Goslin had beaten Manush for the American League batting crown by just one point, .379 to .378. The Browns also kicked in Crowder.

Although Washington did not win the pennant that year, Griffith set the groundwork for the 1933 pennant-winning team. Crowder, Manush, and especially Cronin proved invaluable. In 1928, Griffith had plucked Cronin from Kansas City, a minor league team, for $7,500. But Griffith didn't think much of him at the time. When he told reporters the team had purchased "a young shortstop, name of Cronin," a reporter asked for a first name.

"It don't make no difference, and I don't even know if he's got a first name," Griffith responded. "He's only gonna be around long enough to give (shortstop) Bob Reeves a rest, then we'll ship him to Birmingham. Don't you fellows go writin' your heads off about him now—he's only a fair to middlin' busher." Little did Griffith know that he had himself a future Hall-of-Fame player, manager, and even son-in-law.

In yet another Kansas City bargain, Griffith picked up Joe Kuhel for $65,000 late in the 1930 season. Kuhel took over for Joe Judge at first base the next year, and become yet another key ingredient in the '33 team.

In 1931, Washington put together another good year under Johnson, finishing with a .597 winning percentage. But the team fell to third place as the Yankees claimed second, and the Athletics won 107 games en route to their third straight pennant. Griffith continued to build up the team's starting pitching by purchasing Monte Weaver from the minor league Baltimore team.

Posting its second .600 season in three years, the Senators won 93 games in 1932, but still fell victim to better ball clubs. Its .604 winning percentage ranked just third in the league, as the Yankees this time won the pennant with 107 wins. The Senators finished 14 games back, and one game behind the second-place Athletics.

The new Senators continued to develop. Crowder led the league in wins, going 26–13 with a 3.33 ERA, while Weaver won 22 games. Heinie Manush batted .342 with 14 homers and 116 RBIs. Cronin hit .318 with 116 RBIs, leading the league with 18 triples.

Despite piloting the team to another excellent record, Johnson was fired after the '32 season. The Big Train proved the adage "Nice Guys Finish Last" wrong, but some thought he was too nice to finish first.

"It was believed in many quarters that Johnson was too easy-going to infuse the fighting spirit held so vital to a pennant-winning club," the *Washington Post* wrote after the manager got sacked. Johnson managed the Cleveland Indians the next three seasons, guiding the team to two third-place finishes. In 1940, he ran for Congress from Maryland as a Republican, but lost the race to Democrat William Byron.

Griffith didn't immediately name a replacement for Johnson, and even considered the possibility of returning to the dugout himself "in case of emergency." But the owner soon settled on a new manager, deciding to return to the winning formula of the mid-1920s—a pilot in his mid-20s. Griffith named Joe Cronin player-manager days before the star shortstop's 26th birthday. Cronin was even younger than Bucky Harris, the "Boy Wonder," had been when Harris took over the 1924 Senators.

"I like these scrappy youngsters as leaders," Griffith said, adding that he was enthusiastic about Cronin's "pep and fight and willingness to take a chance."

He maintained realistic expectations for his young manager. "I'm not looking for him to suddenly turn us into a championship team," Griffith said. But once again he underestimated Joe Cronin.

Griffith had other changes in store for the Senators, making a series of key trades before the 1933 season to fortify the team. In yet another blockbuster trade with the St. Louis Browns, Washington swapped outfielders Sam West and Carl Reynolds for outfielders Fred Schulte and former Senator Goslin. Although Goslin wasn't a batting title threat anymore, he had a good year in 1933, batting .297 with 10 triples and 10 home runs. Two pitchers also changed hands in the deal—Washington exchanged Lloyd Brown for Lefty Stewart, who went 15–6 for the '33 Nats.

Griffith also acquired Earl Whitehill from the Tigers, who won 22 games for the 1933 Senators with a 3.33 ERA, and pitcher Jack Kelly from the Indians, who won 12 games and saved a league-high 13, with a svelte 2.69 ERA.

If the Senators were to win the pennant, they would have to dethrone the New York Yankees, just as they had in 1924. The two teams fought it out between the lines—and sometimes outside them.

On April 25, the Yankees and Senators faced off at Griffith Stadium for the third game of a three-game series. Lingering animosity was still pent up from the previous season, when Bill Dickey, the Yankees' catcher, and Carl Reynolds, then a Senators outfielder, had fought it out at home plate.

This time, Yankees base runner Ben Chapman came in spikes flying to break up a double play in the fourth inning, knocking Washington second baseman Buddy Myer's feet out from under him. With Chapman still on the ground, an enraged Myer kicked him several times in the back. The two players exchanged blows as players from both dugouts rushed out to get a piece of the action.

Chapman and Myer were ejected from the game, and Chapman made his way to the Yankee clubhouse. Unfortunately, that required a trip through the Washington dugout, where Senators players didn't exactly greet him with flowers. When Nats pitcher Earl Whitehill made a comment that Chapman found particularly offensive, the Yankee outfielder punched him in the face. Now hundreds of Washington fans stormed onto the field to join the melee. Some got several punches in before Chapman's Yankees teammates could rush to his defense. Police had to come on the field to restore order, arresting five fans, and the game was delayed for 15 minutes. But the Yankees did the only baseball thrashing that day, whipping the Senators, 16–0. American League President Will Harridge fined Chapman, Myer, and Whitehill $100 each and suspended them for five games.

Chapman was unapologetic about instigating the brawl. "That's baseball and always has been, breaking up double plays," he said. "That's what I'm in there for when I'm running. If this game is ping pong, I don't know anything about it. I'm playing baseball."

Washington dropped to 6–6 with the loss, and the Yankees improved to 8–2. The defeat seemed to ignite the Senators, who won eight of their next 10. They also handled the Yankees well that year, winning the season series, 14–8, which helped decide the pennant. The Senators won the flag by seven games over the Yankees, putting together the finest season in Washington history—a 99–53 record, good for a .651 winning percentage.

Four regulars hit .300 or better: first baseman Joe Kuhel (.322 with 107 RBIs), second baseman Buddy Myer (.302 with 15 triples), outfielder Heinie Manush (.336 with 95 RBIs and a league-high 17 triples), and shortstop-manager Cronin (.309 with a team-high 118 RBIs and a league-high 45 doubles). On the mound, Crowder shared the league lead with 24 victories.

Washington's pennant-winning team drew just 437,000 fans that year, an average of 5,757 fans a game, but attendance was way down across baseball because of the Depression. Only the Yankees outdrew it in the American League with 728,000 fans. The St. Louis Browns, by contrast, drew just 88,000 fans for the entire season, for an average of 1,144 fans per game—in what many consider the best baseball town in America! True, St. Louis had two teams back then, but even the more popular Cardinals drew just 256,000 fans.

In the World Series, Washington faced off against the team it had defeated in 1924, the New York Giants. When the teams had last faced each other, Bill Terry was a rookie first baseman for the Giants; now he was their player-manager, and the team's only .300 hitter, with a .322 batting average. But this Giants team was built on pitching.

New York led the National League with an amazing 2.71 ERA, and featured a trio of dominating starting pitchers—southpaw Carl Hubbell, who led the league in wins (23), shutouts (10), and ERA (1.66); Hal Schumacher, who won 19 games with a 2.16 ERA; and "Fat Freddie" Fitzsimmons, who won 16 with a 2.90 ERA.

In the first two games of the series, played in New York's Polo Grounds, Washington managed just three runs against Hubbell and Schumacher, and fell behind, two games to none. Hubbell set the pace quickly in game one by striking

Pennant winners again: the 1933 Washington Senators. Rucker Archive

out the side in the first inning, fanning Myer, Manush, and Goslin, and went the distance in a 4–2 victory over Lefty Stewart (both Nationals runs were unearned). Schumacher also pitched a complete game in New York's 6–1 victory the next day over 24-game winner Alvin Crowder.

When the series returned to Washington for game 3, only 25,727 fans showed up on the rainy afternoon, including President Franklin D. Roosevelt. Those who came were treated to a fine pitching performance by Earl Whitehill in a must-win game for Washington. The first-year Nat mowed down the Giants with a shutout, and the Senators won, 4–0. Leadoff man Buddy Myer went 3-for-4 with a run scored and two RBIs.

The pivotal game of the series would be next. Once again, Washington had the difficult task of facing Hubbell, this time sending Monte Weaver to the mound for his first start of the series. Weaver surrendered a solo home run to Terry in the top of the fourth, but Washington tied it in the bottom of the seventh inning, when Kuhel bunted his way on, moved to second on a sacrifice, and scored on a single by Luke Sewell.

The game went into extra innings, and the two starting pitchers continued to battle. In the top of the 11th, New York went with the small-ball strategy that Washington had used to tie the score four innings earlier. Travis Jackson legged out a bunt, moved 90 feet up on a sacrifice by Gus Mancuso, and scored the go-ahead run on a single by Blondy Ryan, who had hit just .238 in the regular season.

In the bottom of the inning, Washington tried to manufacture the tying run with a similar tactic. Fred Schulte singled to left, and Kuhel reached on a bunt to put runners on first and second with none out. Bluege sacrificed the runners to second and third. The Giants intentionally walked Sewell to load the bases, and Cliff Bolton came in to pinch-hit for pitcher Jack Russell. All Washington needed was a fly ball to tie the game, and a single would likely win it. But Bolton hit a ground ball to shortstop, and the Giants turned it into a game-ending 6-4-3 double play. New York now led the series, 3–1.

In game five, the Giants jumped out to a 2–0 second-inning lead, as the Giants' pitcher, Schumacher, knocked in two runs on a single off Crowder. New York made it 3–0 in the sixth, but Washington rallied to tie the score in the bottom of the frame on a three-run homer by Fred Schulte, triggering memories of the come-from-behind victories by the 1924 World Series team. Schulte had hit only five home runs in the regular season.

For the second straight day, the teams lumbered on into extra innings at Griffith Stadium. Jack Russell, who had come in on relief in the sixth inning, stayed on for Washington in the tenth inning. He surrendered a long drive to center field by Mel Ott. Schulte got a glove on the ball, but it bounced into the stands for a home run, giving the Giants a 4–3 lead.

In the bottom of the inning, the Senators put two men on base with two outs, and Schulte came to the plate with a chance to win the game. But he struck out looking against the Giants' 42-year-old Cuban reliever, Dolf Luque, and the World Series was over. The Senators would never return to another one.

FOUR

RED, WHITE, AND GRAY:
WASHINGTON'S NEGRO LEAGUE TEAM

RED, WHITE, AND GRAY: WASHINGTON'S NEGRO LEAGUE TEAM

Washington may have lost two mediocre major league baseball teams in the last century, but it also picked up a great one. In the late 1930s and through the 1940s, the Homestead Grays of the Negro National League began splitting games between their original home of Homestead, Pennsylvania, and D.C. Within a few years, the Grays played primarily in Washington, providing fans there with an outstanding baseball team at a time when the Senators were struggling. The Grays also shined a spotlight on a missed opportunity for the Nats to both make a historical stand for civil rights and better themselves in the process, because literally playing in the Senators' own ballpark were the "Thunder Twins"—Negro League stars Josh Gibson and Buck Leonard.

Before 1940, several Negro League teams had tried to make a go of it in Washington, but none were successful. The Washington Potomacs lasted just a couple of years in the 1920s, and the Elite Giants decided to skip town for Baltimore after playing in D.C. in 1936 and 1937. There was even a Washington Black Senators team that went 1–20 in 1938 before folding up its tent.

It wasn't that black Washingtonians weren't into baseball. They were, but they enthusiastically supported the Senators, even though major league baseball was closed off to black players. Ironically, Griffith Stadium was located in a black neighborhood, close to Howard University, one of the nation's premier black colleges. But as Washington was a segregated southern city, blacks would sit in their own section of the ballpark, in the right-field pavilion. A famous photograph shows black fans leaning over the railing just inches away from an unconscious Babe Ruth, who had slammed into the wall chasing a ball, on July 5, 1924.

Shirley Povich, who was named sports editor of the *Washington Post* around this time, described 1920s Washington as a "sadly segregated city."

"No newspaper bothered to cover games of the black high schools, and Howard University teams got scant notice," Povich wrote in a retrospective column more than 60 years later. "It was an inconceivable age when blacks were denied service in restaurants, admission to downtown movie theaters and white hotels, and there was almost a common acceptance of that condition that later would call forth such outrage. The civil rights movement was in its early, feeble stage.

Once, after a delegation of black leaders visited the managing editor of *The Post*, he told me of their complaint: They wanted *The Post*, when we used the word Negro in the future, to use it with a capital N."

In 1938, black fans at Griffith Stadium took angry retribution against a Yankees outfielder who had made a violent racial slur. The outfielder, Jake Powell, had been asked in a WGN radio interview what he did in the off-season. Powell responded that he worked as a police officer in Dayton, Ohio, where he particularly enjoyed "cracking niggers over the head." The interview was immediately terminated, and Commissioner Kenesaw Mountain Landis suspended Powell for 10 days.

About two weeks later, Powell made his first start after the suspension in the second game of a doubleheader at Griffith Stadium. Powell had started his career as a Senator, but this was no homecoming. Black fans booed and threw soda bottles at him, causing the game to be delayed for several minutes. One bottle flew right behind Powell's shoulders when he was on first base; a tin pail came close to hitting him. "Take him out! Take him out!" fans chanted from the black section of the ballpark. Despite their taunts, the Yankees swept the doubleheader, 16–1 and 6–2.

Yankees manager Joe McCarthy stood by his decision to play Powell, a platoon player, at Griffith Stadium. "Powell will play in our outfield against southpaw pitching if they throw a million bottles on him," the defiant skipper declared. "I had to send him out there to face the music. Once Powell got in the game, I wouldn't have taken him out if we'd all been killed."

Some accused Commissioner Landis of hypocrisy in suspending Powell for a racist remark, yet presiding over a sport which closed off its ranks to black players. *Washington Post* columnist Westbrook Pegler wrote: "Judge Landis, who tried the case and imposed the penalty, would thus placate the colored clientele of a business which trades under the name of the national game but has always treated the Negroes as Adolph Hitler treats the Jews."

Powell, by the way, was an equal-opportunity bigot. Two years earlier, on April 29, 1936, while still a Senator, he collided with Detroit's Jewish first baseman, Hank Greenberg. Many saw anti-Semitism in Powell's dirty play, which broke Greenberg's wrist, sidelining him for the season. Powell, who retired after the 1945 season, would end his life by committing suicide in a Washington police station while being questioned on a charge of writing bad checks.

Around the time of the Powell incident at Griffith Stadium, black fans in Washington were getting their own team to root for—and a winning one at that. From 1937 to 1945, the Grays won nine straight Negro National League titles. The team's most recognizable stars were catcher Josh Gibson and first baseman Buck Leonard, nicknamed the "black Babe Ruth" and "black Lou Gehrig," respectively. Gibson, like Ruth, was a monstrous home run hitter, and Leonard,

The 1944 Homestead Grays. Rucker Archive

like Gehrig, was an unassuming first baseman with tremendous power. The two usually batted 3-4, just like Ruth and Gehrig did for the Yankees, and were elected to the National Baseball Hall of Fame in 1972.

Gibson and Leonard saw the Senators' games as well. "We went to their games," Leonard told an Associated Press reporter in 1994, three years before his death at age 90. "We watched those boys. We imitated them. We wanted to be just like them."

Another Hall-of-Fame player, Cool Papa Bell, was one of the fastest players ever. Bell joined the Grays in 1943, when he turned 40, and stayed for three seasons. Gibson famously said, "Cool Papa Bell was so fast he could get out of bed, turn out the lights across the room and be back in bed under the covers before the lights went out."

Gibson's heroics were legendary, and some of them were in fact legends. He was said to have hit a ball out of Yankee Stadium in 1934, which would make him the only player to do so, although no documentation exists. But some feats were documented. At a doubleheader at Griffith Stadium in 1939 he hit three home runs and a triple. One home run "followed the left-field foul line until it went out of sight," the *Post* reported. In 1937, he hit a ball that traveled 580 feet at Yankee Stadium. Once, in a game in Monessen, Pennsylvania, he hit a ball so far over the center-field fence that the mayor stopped the game to measure it, at 512 feet.

Josh Gibson, said to be the greatest power hitter of all time, swings the bat.
Rucker Archive

"Josh's power came almost completely from strength above his waist: arms, shoulders, and back muscles so awesome that he didn't need the coiled power of his legs or the whiplike action of his wrists," wrote William Brashler in *Josh Gibson: A Life in the Negro Leagues.* "With his upper-body power, he could thrash a ball with a motion much like that of beating a rug. He stood flat-footed, his heavy bat gripped down to the end and held high above his right shoulder, his feet spread fairly wide apart, and with the pitch he strode only slightly—some say about four inches, some say not at all, but simply raised his foot and put it down in the same spot when the pitch came."

Gibson started his career with the Grays but left to play for several seasons in the 1930s with the rival Pittsburgh Crawfords before returning to his original team. Years later Leonard would describe the unique defensive shift the Grays would employ against the right-handed-hitting Gibson. The corner outfielders would play toward the gaps, the first baseman and third baseman would play away from the foul lines, and the middle infielders would play deep, Leonard wrote in a 1970 *Washington Star* story with Negro League historian John Holway.

"And then the pitcher would throw the ball straight down the middle of the plate," Leonard said. "He could hit the ball 500 feet to center field and we would catch it—I say 500 feet, but I mean extreme center. We'd gang up right in the center. He couldn't pull it—not a fastball. Throw it straight down the middle of the plate, and just hope we catch it, because he's going to hit it 400-something feet."

Gibson's Hall of Fame plaque states that the slugger hit nearly 800 home runs in league and independent games and won four Negro National League batting titles. The most impressive came in 1943, when Gibson hit a ridiculous .517, as well as more home runs at spacious Griffith Stadium than the entire Senators team did that year. In exhibition at-bats against major league pitchers, in fact, Gibson batted .426. At six feet one, 215 pounds, Gibson had the build of a catcher, but his defense was not his strong suit. He had trouble with pop-ups, although he had a cannon for an arm.

For all his hitting prowess, one pitcher had his number: Satchel Paige. At a game in Pittsburgh in 1942 with a runner on third base, the theatrical Paige walked two men intentionally to face Gibson with the bases loaded. "Three fastballs, Josh," Paige said, before fanning the Grays' slugger on three pitches.

When the Grays met Paige's Kansas City Monarchs for the Negro World Series that year, Gibson again came up with the bases loaded, and this time with a chance to tie the game, as the Monarchs led 8–4. But Paige repeated his earlier feat, striking out Gibson on three pitches, and the Monarchs swept the four-game series.

Gibson scores. Rucker Archive

Leonard, meanwhile, was the glue of the Grays' franchise, especially during the 1940–41 seasons, when Gibson played in Venezuela and Mexico for higher wages. Leonard was such a good fastball hitter that Monte Irvin, who would star in both the Negro Leagues and the major leagues, once said, "Trying to sneak a fastball past him was like trying to sneak a sunrise past a rooster."

A lifetime .341 hitter, Leonard averaged 34 home runs a year, once hitting as many as 42 homers in a season. He was also an outstanding defensive first baseman. And unlike Gibson, who was a heavy drinker, Leonard did not consume alcohol.

In 1942, the two stars held out until they got $1,000 a month for the five-month season. "When I started out with the Grays in 1934, I was getting $125 a month—for 4½ months," Leonard wrote in the *Washington Star* article. "My best payday was 1948; I made $10,000 that year all told, summer and winter. And baseball was a rough life back then. We'd play 210 games a year, then go to Cuba or Puerto Rico all winter and play winter ball."

Back then, in addition to league games, Negro League teams played exhibition games against semipro ball clubs—both black and white—and would go on barnstorming trips in the off-season.

One of the most celebrated interracial exhibition games took place on May 31, 1942, when Satchel Paige joined the Grays for a day as they took on the Dizzy Dean All-Stars, a major league team headlined by the former Cardinals pitching star. A crowd of 22,000 fans, more than quadruple the average Senators attendance that season, came out to Griffith Stadium to see the matchup. Dean, who had retired the previous season, pitched just the first inning, surrendering two runs. Paige, meanwhile, gave up one run in five innings, striking out seven, as the Grays won, 8–1. The rush for tickets so overwhelmed the ballpark staff that some fans couldn't get into the stadium until the fourth inning, when Dean was long gone.

The Grays were becoming a hot ticket in Washington, especially when Paige came to town. Three weeks later, Paige returned to Griffith Stadium, but this time in an enemy uniform, as his Kansas City Monarchs took on the Grays. Twenty-eight thousand fans packed the ballpark for the 9 p.m. game. Paige held the Grays scoreless in his five innings of work, but the Grays' pitcher, Roy Partlow, did him four better, pitching nine scoreless frames. In the top of the tenth, Partlow finally surrendered the game's first run as Kansas City took a 1–0 lead. In the bottom of the inning, the Grays tied the score, and then Partlow won it with an RBI triple. The crowd rushed on to the field to carry him off in celebration.

A Negro League game at Griffith Stadium in Washington. Rucker Archive

Around this time, Clark Griffith arranged for a meeting with the Grays' two superstars, Leonard and Gibson. The Senators' owner called them to his office after a Grays game, Leonard recalled in the *Star* article. The conversation went like this:

"You fellows got good size on you and you looked like you were playing to win," Griffith said, before telling the players of pressure from black sportswriters to put them on his team. "Well, let me tell you something: If we get you boys, we're going to get the best ones. It's going to break up your league. Now what do you think of all that?"

The players told Griffith that they hadn't given it much thought. They said they'd be happy to play in the major leagues, but that they'd leave it to others to make a case for them.

"Well, I just wanted to see how you fellows felt about it," Griffith said.

Publicly, Griffith was singing the praises of the players as well. Two days before the Grays-Monarchs June 1942 showdown, Griffith said of Gibson, "There's a catcher worth $150,000 of anybody's money right now. If I could have had him I'd have gone after him some time ago." Griffith added that Gibson was as good as Hall-of-Fame catchers Bill Dickey, Mickey Cochrane, and Gabby Hartnett.

Of course, Griffith could have had Gibson at any time, if the Senators' owner had been willing to challenge baseball's color barrier.

By all accounts, Griffith was not a racist. He opened the stadium to black community events, and was made an honorary deacon by Elder Solomon Lightfoot Michaux of the neighboring Church of God, which held religious services at Griffith Stadium, according to Brad Snyder's detailed history of the Grays, *Beyond the Shadow of the Senators*.

"Most black Washingtonians considered Griffith—in contrast to the virulently racist Redskins owner George Preston Marshall—a friend," Snyder wrote.

But Griffith had a financial stake in keeping the Grays afloat, receiving rent from the team, which helped him subsidize his own losing ball club. Still, one has to wonder whether Leonard and Gibson could have helped turn the Senators into both a winning team and a profitable one. From 1939 to 1945, the Senators averaged more than 8,000 fans a game only once, and twice averaged less than 5,000 fans. The team did pull off two surprise second-place finishes during this period, but otherwise finished sixth twice, seventh twice, and eighth (last) once.

Griffith's meeting with Leonard and Gibson followed years of intense lobbying by black sportswriter Sam Lacy of the *Baltimore Afro-American*, who was joined in his crusade to integrate baseball by fellow African-American journalists Wendell Smith of the *Pittsburgh Courier* and Joe Bostic of the *People's Voice* in Harlem.

Lacy grew up in Washington, the grandson of the first black detective on the Washington police force, Henry Erskine Lacy. Lacy's father was a passionate fan of the Washington Senators, and the young Lacy worked as a vendor at

Griffith Stadium, watching the white stars of the day. Meanwhile, he would play semipro baseball with other black players, including Negro Leaguers.

"I was in a position to make some comparisons, and it seemed to me that those black players were good enough to play in the big leagues," Lacy said in a *Sports Illustrated* interview in 1990, 13 years before his death at age 99. "There was, of course, no talk then of that ever happening. When I was growing up, there was no real opportunity for blacks in any sport. It never crossed our minds as kids to aspire to the big leagues. Even the best players considered it a lost cause. But the idea stuck with me. I felt that not only were blacks being deprived of the opportunity to make some money but that whites were being deprived of the opportunity to see these fellows perform. I could see that both were being cheated. And so, with a certain amount of ego, I took it upon myself to be the wedge."

In 1935, a full dozen years before Jackie Robinson broke baseball's color barrier, Lacy wrote a column in the *Washington Tribune*, a black weekly newspaper, urging baseball to integrate. "If baseball club-owners are really anxious to come to their own rescue, they should put a little 'color' in the game," he wrote.

Two years later, Lacy met with Griffith, and quoted the Senators owner as saying, "The time is not far off when colored players will take their places beside those of the other races in the major leagues. However, I am not so sure that time has arrived yet." Griffith also called on Negro teams to organize themselves into a legitimate, professionally-run league, and predicted, accurately, that the first black player would be subject to "cruel, filthy epithets."

Lacy's own father had experienced that firsthand by a Washington Senators player. In the *Sports Illustrated* interview, Lacy recalled how his father came out to cheer the Senators for an opening-day parade in the 1920s:

"And so there he was, age seventy-nine, out there cheering with the rest of them, calling all the players by name, just happy to be there. And then it happened. One of the white players—I won't say which one—just gave him this nasty look and, as he passed by, spat right in his face. Right in that nice old man's face. That hurt my father terribly. And you know, as big a fan as he had been, he never went to another game as long as he lived, which was seven more years."

The 1948 Homestead Grays. Rucker Archive

Although Clark Griffith had voiced some encouraging words back in 1937, as years went by he did nothing to integrate the team. According to Griffith's adopted son, Calvin, the Senators owner was talking with the Grays' ownership about having black teams take on major league teams.

"There were two brothers that owned the Grays. And they were talking to Mr. Griffith about one of these days they wanted to challenge the major leagues for the championship," Calvin Griffith told biographer Jon Kerr years later in *Baseball's Last Dinosaur*. "And that's the only reason Mr. Griffith didn't sign some of 'em. But Branch Rickey went out and broke it all up by signing Jackie Robinson. If he hadn't signed Jackie Robinson there could have been in the years to come a challenge of the black to the white."

The idea of integrating baseball while keeping teams segregated was discussed openly back in the 1940s. Satchel Paige endorsed the idea, but Lacy ridiculed it.

"Paige's proposal that a colored team be admitted to one or both of the big leagues, as an entity, is foolish," Lacy wrote in a 1942 column. "There can be no compromise with prejudice. Unless Negro players are infiltrated the same situation will exist. A separate club for Negroes is no more logical than a separate team for Italians, Irishmen, Germans, Poles, Lithuanians or Jews."

Meanwhile, Leonard and Gibson never heard back from Griffith after their meeting. "I always thought the Senators might be first to take a Negro, because Washington was about half-Negro then," Leonard wrote in 1970. "But Griffith was always looking for Cuban ballplayers."

Griffith's penchant for finding low-cost Cuban ballplayers dated to his days as manager of the Cincinnati Reds. In 1911, he signed two Cubans, Armando Marsans and Rafael Almeida. But it was an opposing Cuban player that really motivated Griffith to start scouting on the Caribbean island.

In the 1933 World Series between the Senators and the New York Giants, the teams were tied 3–3 in the sixth inning of game five when the Giants sent in their 42-year-old reliever, Dolf Luque. The Havana native held the Nats scoreless for 4⅓ innings, allowing the Giants to win the game, 4–3, in 10 innings, and claim the series, four games to one. Luque struck out five Senators and surrendered just two hits in getting the victory. He retired two years later with a lifetime 3.24 ERA.

Griffith hired Joe Cambria, a former minor league ballplayer and Baltimore laundry business owner, and suggested he trawl Cuba for prospects. Cambria, who had moved with his parents to the United States from Italy when he was just three months old, helped Griffith open a pipeline to inexpensive Cuban talent. He also owned a Negro League team, the Baltimore Black Sox, as well as a host of minor league teams.

"Papa Joe" Cambria, a familiar figure in his straw hats, became so well known in Cuba that a Havana cigar was named for him. He went on to sign four hundred Cuban players over the years, in addition to Americans such as Mickey

Vernon and Ed Yost. Among his most notable Cuban finds were pitchers Camilo Pascual, Pedro Ramos, Conrado Marrero, Roberto Estalella, and outfielder Tony Oliva, who signed with the team after it moved to Minnesota. Cambria once even scouted pitcher Fidel Castro at Havana University, but concluded the future dictator had a good curveball but not enough zip on his fastball.

Even as Griffith resisted integrating baseball with American-born black players, he skirted the color barrier by signing tan-skinned Cubans who could pass as white. "There's no question that some of the ballplayers Mr. Griffith signed had black blood," Calvin Griffith told Kerr. "But nobody said anything about it. Nobody said nothing about it. So why bring up questions about something that nobody asked about?"

The players faced rough treatment on the field and discrimination off it. "The Cuban ballplayers, some of them were as black as your tape recorder," Calvin Griffith told Snyder in an interview a few years before his death. "We had to find places for them to stay across the railroad tracks."

On June 24, 1945, a highly touted rookie with the Kansas City Monarchs came to Washington for a game against the Grays. The *Post* called shortstop Jackie Robinson "amazingly agile" and "a smooth and graceful defensive man" with one of the best arms in baseball. Eighteen thousand fans came out for the doubleheader, more than double the Senators' average crowd that year.

Robinson gave the Monarchs a 1–0 lead in the first inning of the opening game by doubling and scoring, but the Grays stormed back to take the opener, 11–3, over Satchel Paige, and also won the second game, 10–6. Four months later, when Brooklyn Dodgers President Branch Rickey signed Robinson to a contract with the Dodgers, Clark Griffith became one of the deal's harshest critics.

Griffith did not say that blacks did not belong in the game. Instead, the Senators' owner argued that Rickey was wrong to pluck Robinson off the Kansas City Monarchs' roster without compensating the team.

"While it is true that we have no agreement with Negro leagues—National and American—we still can't act like outlaws in taking their stars," Griffith said. "If Brooklyn wanted to buy Robinson from Kansas City, that would be all right, but contracts of Negro teams should be recognized by organized baseball."

Griffith, who ironically had traded for a young Rickey 40 years earlier as manager of the New York Highlanders, now engaged in a testy public debate with his former player. "There is no Negro league as such as far as I am concerned," Rickey responded. "Negro baseball is in the zone of a racket and there is not a circuit that could be admitted to organized baseball, Clark Griffith of Washington to the contrary."

Rickey also charged that Griffith had signed Cuban players who were themselves black, a strange charge coming from a man who was integrating baseball. Griffith's response was equally bizarre: "Cuban ballplayers have always been acceptable in organized baseball, and so far as I am concerned no racial problem is involved."

In 1946, as Robinson was making his professional debut at the Dodgers' minor league team in Montreal, Josh Gibson was playing his final season. Gibson, now 34, was overweight and suffering from high blood pressure and the ill effects of excessive drinking—and possibly drug use. He died the following January of a stroke at the age of 35, just three months before Robinson broke baseball's color barrier.

"Gibson was so good if he was in the major leagues they would have to say that he was the best catcher that ever caught," Calvin Griffith told Kerr. "That's how good he was. He could sit on his ass and throw the ball to second base better than anybody standing up."

The Grays trudged on even after blacks started playing in the major leagues, but the fans' interest, understandably, waned considerably. "We couldn't draw flies," Leonard said. The team played its final game ever at Griffith Stadium in 1950, with old nemesis Satchel Paige fittingly on the mound for the opposing Philadelphia Stars. Paige had made his major league debut with the Cleveland Indians in 1948, but returned to the pitch in the Negro Leagues in 1950 before rejoining the big leagues in 1951 with the St. Louis Browns. This time the Grays got the better of Paige, winning 7–1. They finished the season 100–26 after winning their final game ever, on the road in West Virginia.

But when the 1951 season began, there were still no black players on the Senators. So Washington's African-American fans cheered visiting black players, such as Larry Doby of the Cleveland Indians. Doby, the first black player in American League history, broke in just three months after Jackie Robinson, and faced much of the same abuse as his predecessor. But he had a good experience playing on the road in Washington, one of the southernmost cities in the league.

"When people say, 'You played well in Washington,' well, I had a motivation factor there," Doby recalled in a 1997 interview with the *Post*. "I had cheerleaders there at Griffith Stadium. I didn't have to worry about name-calling. You got cheers from those people when you walked out onto the field. They'd let you know they appreciated you were there. Give you a little clap when you go out there, and if you hit a home run, they'd acknowledge the fact, tip their hat."

In 1952, Griffith defensively addressed the issue of why the Senators still had not signed a black player. "My own position with regard to Negro players on a Washington club has come in for criticism and discussion which has not been fair to me," Griffith, by then 82 years old, wrote in a retrospective piece for the *Sporting News*. "To those who persist in speaking of me harshly on the Negro player issue, let me say that I would welcome the addition of players like Robinson, (Roy) Campanella, Harry Simpson, Don Newcombe, Larry Doby and Orestes (Minnie) Minoso to the Washington roster.

"I stand ready, and eager, to place Negro players on our Washington club. But they must rate the jobs on the basis of ability, and not merely because they happen to be Negroes. I will not sign a Negro for the Washington club merely to satisfy subversive persons. I would welcome a Negro on the Senators if he rated the distinction, if he belonged among major league players.

"The Washington club has a large Negro clientele. It represents some of the best citizenship of the District of Columbia. I would only be too glad to give that clientele a chance to root for a player of its own race."

Two more years went by before Washington finally signed a black player. In 1954, Griffith turned to the island that had been the source of so many players—Cuba—to sign Carlos Paula, a black outfielder. Paula would last only three seasons before he was out of baseball. Washington was thus one of the last teams to integrate—only the Yankees, Phillies, Tigers, and Red Sox took longer.

Clark Griffith died in 1955, and his adopted son, Calvin Griffith, took over the team. In 1961, the new owner moved the team to Minneapolis. Seventeen years later, at a Rotary club speech in Waseca, Minnesota, he said, "Black people don't go to ballgames, but they'll fill up a rassling ring and put up such a chant they'll scare you to death. We came (to Minnesota) because you've got good, hard-working white people here."

The *Minneapolis Star* called for Griffith to sell the team, and civil rights groups called for a boycott of Twins games. Twins star Rod Carew fumed, "I'm not going to be another nigger on his plantation," and was traded after the season to the California Angels.

"The words were misunderstood, taken out of context. I had had a couple of drinks and was trying to be funny," said Griffith, adding he did not know a reporter was present.

He told Kerr that it was "one of the worst things I ever went through. I went down there to play golf and go to a dinner. But they got a writer there that had to be sensational and intimated things I didn't say. I was shocked as hell."

Griffith recalled his interaction with black fans in Washington, when he oversaw Griffith Stadium during Grays games as Senators vice president.

"How could I talk about blacks when our ballpark had 350,000 of 'em every year and I practically knew half of them," he said. "They've been good to us. They were our bread-and-butter in Washington. The Homestead Grays brought in money all summer—fourteen games or so. You're not gonna knock anybody that kept you alive."

Carew and Griffith later patched things up.

"I can't say there was a racist bone in his body," Carew said when Griffith died. "Look at all the Latin American and African-American players he signed and helped. I think some of the things he said came out wrong. I was upset at the time and said some things. Later, I thought it over and apologized to him for what I said."

FIVE

HAIL TO THE PITCH:
PRESIDENTS AND SENATORS

HAIL TO THE PITCH: PRESIDENTS AND SENATORS

On April 14, 2005, President George W. Bush achieved something that Presidents Bill Clinton, George H. W. Bush, Jimmy Carter, and Gerald Ford couldn't—he threw out the first ball at a Washington baseball game. It had been 36 years since Richard Nixon's opening-day toss in 1969. But Bush's pitch looked far different than those made at old Senators games. In the 20th century, presidents showed up in a suit and tie, sometimes encumbered by an overcoat, and threw the ball from the stands.

Sporting a Nationals jacket, Bush let it rip from the pitcher's mound at RFK.

Presidential tosses at Washington baseball games date back to 1910, with William Howard Taft, and continued with every president throwing out at least one opening-day pitch in the nation's capital until the city was left without a team in 1972.

While most presidents relished the opportunity to get a photo-op at the national pastime, not every national leader was a baseball fan. Taft's predecessor, Teddy Roosevelt, scorned baseball as a "mollycoddle game." (For those not up on their early 1900s lingo, "mollycoddle" means pampered or overprotected.) In 1907, a delegation from the National Association of Professional Baseball Leagues presented Roosevelt with a season pass, made of solid 14-karat gold, "to recognize your practical support of a game that nourishes no 'mollycoddles.'" Hey, at least these guys had a sense of humor.

Taft, who at 330 pounds was the size of catcher and infielder combined, took a greater liking to the sport. On April 14, 1910, he started the first-pitch tradition by tossing one to Senators pitcher Walter Johnson, who went on to hurl a one-hit shutout against the Philadelphia Athletics. It was Taft's presence that indirectly cost Johnson a no-hitter. Washington outfielder Doc Gessler later admitted that when a fly ball was hit in his direction, he had been daydreaming of hitting a grand slam and talking to the president about it. Backing up, Gessler tripped over a fan (spectators could stand on the field behind a rope back then) and the ball dropped for a double.

By 1912, the Senators had a new manager and part-owner, Clark Griffith. Taft couldn't make the opening game that year, due to the sinking of the *Titanic* four days earlier. But Griffith wanted to keep a good marketing tradition afloat.

President William Howard Taft starts a tradition by throwing out the first pitch on opening day, April 14, 1910. Rucker Archives

"It occurred to me that this would be a fine annual custom," Griffith wrote in a 1955 *Washington Star* piece called "Presidents Who Have Pitched for Me." "So I requested a meeting with him (Taft) and he received me very amiably. 'I'd like to establish this as an annual function,' I told him, 'and if you would cooperate it might catch on.'"

Taft's reply, according to Griffith: "Why sure, Griff. I'll be glad to start the ball rolling."

So began Griffith's long string of relationships with presidents all the way through Dwight Eisenhower. The owner's office was adorned with pictures of presidents throwing out the first ball at Griffith Stadium, and Griffith befriended not just presidents, but Supreme Court justices, cabinet members, and real senators.

Although 1912 was just Griffith's first year in Washington, he already knew something about presidents and baseball. In 1908, as manager of the New York Highlanders (later renamed the Yankees), Griffith had visited the White House in Roosevelt's final year as president. With opening day already past in 1912, Griffith arranged for Taft to throw out the first pitch two months later, on June 18. Taft was "merry with enthusiasm," according to a *Washington Post* story the next day. A crowd of 15,516 fans, the second-largest in Washington history to that point, came out to see the Senators win their 17th straight game, a 5–4 victory over the Athletics. It was a great year for the Washington Senators. They finished in second place with a .599 percentage, their first winning season after eleven straight losing records.

Taft's pitch was made to the umpire, not the pitcher. Soon, a new tradition would evolve at Nationals games. Sitting from his box, the president would toss the ball over a scrum of photographers into a crowd of players from both teams, who would battle for it like bridesmaids trying to catch a bouquet. Washington would usually start its season a day before the rest of the American League in what became known as the presidential opener, and Congress would recess for the day so members could catch the president throwing out the first ball.

Taft's successor, Woodrow Wilson, was one of the most enthusiastic baseball fans to occupy the Oval Office. He had a "dugout" at the White House where he read and talked baseball. Even after he left office, Wilson continued to attend games, perhaps in the sweetest seats in baseball history. Griffith recalled that Wilson, who had suffered a stroke that left him partially paralyzed, asked about coming to games, but Griffith was worried about how to accommodate him.

"Finally, I got an idea," the Nationals' owner wrote. "I phoned the president of the American League and asked him for permission to have Mr. Wilson's automobile driven onto the field and parked outside the right-field foul line. 'Well,' he said, 'that might interfere with the right fielder, but if the umpires will sanction it, it's all right with me.'

"I got in touch with the umpires, and they gave me permission. Mr. Wilson's car was parked between the foul line and the seats, and I stationed a player out there to sit on the bumper of the car and ward off any foul balls that might be headed for the automobile."

Griffith made no mention of any dents to Wilson's car.

At the 1922 opener, President Warren Harding, a former minor league team owner, called over Walter Johnson's son, who sat in the president's lap in the first inning. "This is a mighty fine boy you have here," Harding told the pitcher. But Griffith saw something else: a person worn down by the presidency.

"The man who threw the ball out in 1922 looked and acted twenty years older than the man who had so confidently and vigorously thrown the ball the year before," Griffith wrote. "It was not a great surprise to me that Harding did not live to finish his one term."

Calvin Coolidge wasn't much of a baseball fan, but he had to fake it. The Senators won their only World Series during his presidency, in 1924, and the team was a national sensation. Coolidge became the first president to attend a World Series opener, where he threw out the first ball. But it was his wife, Grace, who was the real fan in the first family. She kept score during the World Series games and kept her husband in the game.

President Herbert Hoover had the unfortunate distinction of throwing out a first ball during the Great Depression, during Prohibition, and perhaps worst of all, in Philadelphia. Hoover was booed during a World Series game between the St. Louis Cardinals and the Philadelphia Athletics, whose fans started chanting, "We want beer!" The Athletics have since moved on, and most of those fans are dead, but Philadelphia fans are still known as the toughest crowd, once even booing Santa Claus.

"I left the ball park with the chant of the crowd ringing in my ears: 'We want beer!'" Hoover wrote in his memoirs.

Opening day at Griffith Stadium was a place to be seen for the Washington elite. Newspaper stories would showcase dozens of members of the city's who's who, from the president to senators (real ones), cabinet members, generals, and family members. A 1935 *Washington Post* opening-day story put it this way: "It was all very much like a spectacle outside an ancient Roman arena, where senators, statesmen and military men forgot their dignity in the scuffle to see the famous chariot race between the world's most famous gladiators."

FDR tosses out the first pitch on opening day in 1934. Senators owner, Clark Griffith is pictured to the right of FDR. Rucker Archives

The next year, President Franklin D. Roosevelt made his third opening-day appearance as the Nationals topped the Yankees, 1–0. The Associated Press captured a series of photos of Roosevelt at the ballpark, clearly enjoying himself as he motions with his fingers, looks up in the sky to track a pop-up or fly ball, and flashes a grin.

But his charisma proved to be dangerous. Senators pitcher Bobo Newsom pitched a four-hit shutout that afternoon, despite suffering a broken jaw when a throw by his own third baseman, Ossie Bluege, nailed him in the face. Newsom and Bluege had converged on a bunt, and while Bluege fielded it, Newsom took his eye off the ball to glance at FDR in the stands.

Security wasn't as tight as it is today. Still, the presence of Secret Service agents at a baseball game was an unusual sight, and it prompted this flip description in the *Washington Post* for one of FDR's visits:

"A group of grim-lipped, steel-eyed huskies, all wearing their right hands in their pockets with the nonchalance of long practice, slither past the Washington dugout to the president's box. . . . The Secret Service men are as taut as greyhounds in the starting box. A reporter reaches in his pocket for a cigarette and his hand is jerked away before he can get it. . . . Finally the presidential heave takes place, and there ensues the maddest scramble you ever saw for the ball. Ball players, news photographers, cameramen, reporters and a few civilians pile up like sandlot football players."

In 1940, Roosevelt literally threw a wild pitch, as his opening-day toss slammed into a *Washington Post* photographer's camera. "It was one of the worst that ever left a presidential arm," the *Post* reported, "and that is saying something, for Hoover, Coolidge, Harding and Wilson also heaved some wild ones."

In all, Roosevelt threw out a record eight opening-day pitches. But he had a much more important role in helping to preserve baseball during World War II. Shortly after Pearl Harbor, the baseball commissioner, Judge Kenesaw Mountain Landis, wrote to FDR to get his views on whether baseball should be played during the war.

"If you feel we ought to continue, we would be delighted to do so," Landis wrote. "We await your order." On January 15, 1942, barely a month after Pearl Harbor, Roosevelt responded in what became known as the "Green Light Letter." In it, the president said it would be best for baseball to continue.

"There will be fewer people unemployed and everybody will work longer hours and harder than ever before. And that means that they ought to have a chance for recreation and for taking their minds off their work even more than before," FDR wrote. He also made a pitch for more night baseball, still pretty rare at the time, "because it gives an opportunity to the day shift to see a game occasionally."

FDR made it clear that baseball should not be exempt from the draft: "As to the players themselves, I know you agree with me that the individual players who are active military or naval age should go, without question, into the services. Even if the actual quality to the teams is lowered by the greater use of older players, this will not dampen the popularity of the sport."

Despite the appearance of a cordial correspondence, the two men disliked each other. It was Clark Griffith, a friend of the president, who laid the groundwork for the deal, according to Bill Gilbert's book *The Seasons: Ten Memorable Years in Baseball and in America*.

FDR would not throw another ball out after that. Baseball might have been a good leisure outlet for a country at war, but for a wartime president there were obviously more pressing responsibilities. By the time World War II ended in 1945, FDR was dead. But his successor, Harry Truman, made a point of returning to Griffith Stadium just six days after the Japanese surrender was formalized.

In the midst of a pennant race, Truman arrived at the ballpark on September 8, 1945, to throw out the first ball in a game between the Senators and the St. Louis Browns. Washington won the game 4–1, in front of 20,310 fans, a large crowd for those days. The Senators finished 1½ games out of first that year, in what would be their last serious pennant run. In all, Truman attended 16 games at Griffith Stadium, more than any other president, according to *Baseball: The President's Game*, by William B. Mead and Paul Dickson.

Truman was the first southpaw to throw out a ball at Griffith Stadium, but he sometimes tried to throw right-handed. At the 1950 opener, Griffith placed a second ball in the president's right hand, and Truman threw both balls. Here's how the *Washington Post* assessed the performance: "The first, thrown with his left, was a good one with some loft. It was caught by pitcher Joe Haynes. The right-handed toss was a miserable thing that landed on the turf."

Things were worse for Truman the next year. His appearance at the team's home opener on April 20, 1951, came the day after General Douglas MacArthur spoke before a joint session of Congress, in which he delivered his famous line, "Old soldiers never die, they just fade away." Truman had fired the popular MacArthur as Far East commander earlier that month, and the president was met by a cascade of boos at the ballpark. In an attempt to drown them out, the Air Force Band played "Ruffles and Flourishes" and "Hail to the Chief."

Truman befriended Griffith, and in 1959, six years after Truman had left the White House, he sent Griffith a telegram on the eve of opening day, on which Vice President Richard Nixon was to throw out the first ball: "BEST OF LUCK TO YOU ON OPENING DAY AND EVERY DAY. WATCH OUT FOR THAT NIXON. DON'T LET HIM THROW YOU A CURVE. YOUR FRIEND, HARRY TRUMAN."

In his first year in office, President Dwight D. Eisenhower decided to blow off the 1953 opener so he could go golfing in Augusta, Georgia, infuriating an important voting group—baseball fans. But the game was rained out, so Ike flew back in time to throw the first pitch at the rescheduled opener against the New York Yankees. He stayed for just 1½ innings before flying back to his golfing trip. The Senators lost 6–3.

"President Ike gave us a bad scare because opening day conflicted with a golfing date he had in Atlanta," Griffith wrote two years later. "We were rescued at the last moment by the weather."

Eisenhower was a fan of the game, despite engaging in what might be called "Golfgate" today. "When I was a small boy in Kansas," he once said, "a friend of mine and I went fishing and as we sat there in the warmth of the summer afternoon on a river bank, we talked about what we wanted to do when we grew up. I told him that I wanted to be a real major league baseball player, a genuine professional like Honus Wagner. My friend said that he'd like to be president of the United States. Neither of us got our wish."

Ike got a chance to redeem himself the following season, in 1954. After Mickey Vernon's tenth-inning home run gave the Nats a 5–3 victory over the Yankees, the president got so excited that he started to make his way to the field to congratulate Vernon before Secret Service agents intercepted him. Instead, they brought Vernon over to the president's box. "Wonderful, a wonderful home run," Eisenhower told him.

Meanwhile, First Lady Mamie Eisenhower hugged and kissed Griffith. "What an opener!" Griffith told reporters after the game. "We never had one like it—we never had a president practically run out onto the field to salute one of our ballplayers."

Vernon recalls that as he crossed the plate, someone grabbed at him. "I tried to pull away from him; there was a bunch of players there, and I thought he was just a guy from the stands," Vernon says. "He says, 'No, come with me, the president wants to talk to you.' So he took me over to his box."

Charlie Brotman, longtime public address announcer for the Senators, recalls irking Eisenhower at the home opener in 1956. In the fifth inning the Senators brought in a relief pitcher, but Brotman couldn't see the pitcher's number as he made his way to the mound:

"So one of the guys next to me said, 'I think it's Truman Clevenger. So I said, OK, 'Ladies and gentleman, now coming in to pitch for Washington, Truman . . .' but now he's motioning me to stop. So I turned off the mike and said, 'What's the matter?'

"And he said, 'I don't think it's him.' Meanwhile, the word 'Truman' is just hanging out. I wish I could grab it, bring it back, put it in my pocket, but it is out there. It's just 'Truman.' Meanwhile, I'm looking around to see who else I could ask, and there's nobody. And here's the president of the United States, down in the presidential box, and he starts to look over his left shoulder. And I'm imagining him thinking, 'What is this, some kind big joke or something? Truman preceded me as president. Is President Truman going to come in and pitch for Washington? Is this a joke?'

"Meanwhile, 27,000 people are looking at the president, and the president is looking at me, which made all the spectators look at me. I'm huddling down so that nobody can see me. And I thought, 'This is going to be my first and last game. They're going to fire me.' Finally, the pitcher reached the pitcher's mound, and he got the rosin bag, and I can see that it was Truman Clevenger. Meanwhile, about 20 seconds had passed. In my mind, it was at least 20 minutes. So I just said 'Clevenger.' And that was my first game, and probably my most embarrassing moment."

Despite the mishap, Brotman not only kept his job but must have even impressed one of Ike's men. That fall, someone from the White House called Brotman to see if he would like to introduce the president at the inaugural parade the next year. Brotman has announced every inaugural parade since, most recently George W. Bush's in 2005—15 and counting. "And it all stemmed from baseball," he says.

"What I discovered is that the president's personality really reflected on the parades and the appearances at the ballpark," Bortman says. "Eisenhower couldn't care less about parades, couldn't care less about baseball. It was really no big deal. If anything, it's an intrusion. And so he hoped it would be over with in ten minutes. Kennedy was just the opposite. Kennedy's personality came out. He was very gregarious. He'd shake everybody's hand. And same thing with Nixon. But Johnson played it straight and wanted to get it over with."

In 1960, Eisenhower's final year as president, Ike again took off on a golfing trip to Augusta at the beginning of the baseball season, but this time made a point of interrupting the vacation to fly back to Washington to throw out the season-opening pitch. Washington beat the Boston Red Sox, 10–1, as Camilo Pascual struck out 15 batters, giving Eisenhower a winning record at opening-day games.

"Now that makes me four and three," Ike said after the game.

"That's better than .500 and that's OK in baseball," responded Vice President Nixon.

The next year there was a new president and a new team. John F. Kennedy threw out the first pitch at the 1961 opener, inaugurating the expansion Washington Senators. The old team had moved to Minnesota after the 1960 season to become the Twins. JFK got a rather rude reception on his first pitch as president. White Sox outfielder Jim Rivera, who had snagged the opening toss, was brought over to the box to get the ball signed, in keeping with tradition.

According to a story by *Chicago Tribune* writer David Condon years later, "Jungle Jim" looked at the autographed ball and demanded, "What kind of garbage college is that Harvard, where they don't even teach you to write? What kind of garbage writing is this? What is this garbage autograph? Do you think I can go into any tavern on Chicago's South Side and really say the president of the United States signed this baseball for me? I'd be run off. Take this thing back and give me something besides your garbage autograph."

Laughing the entire time, the young president agreed to sign the ball more legibly.

"You know," Rivera replied, "you're all right."

The Senators lost that game, 4–3, but Kennedy proved a good luck charm the next year, as Washington defeated the Detroit Tigers, 4–1, at the first game ever at its new $23 million D.C. Stadium—the ballpark that would be renamed for Kennedy's brother, Robert F. Kennedy, in 1969.

"I'm leaving you in first place," the president told team owner Pete Quesada and general manager Ed Doherty, but the Kennedy magic was short-lived. The Senators finished in last place.

President John Kennedy overlapped with Washington Senators infielder John Kennedy. The two men even shared the same birthday, May 29. The Kennedy who played for Washington from 1962 to 1964 says he never got a chance to meet the president. But the post office once got their mail mixed up.

"My girlfriend wrote me a letter, and it went to the White House," he recalls. "The post office saw the name John Kennedy, and automatically sent it there. When I went to the ballpark, there was manila envelope waiting for me from the White House."

Kennedy's vice president, Lyndon Johnson, made a famous quip mixing baseball, religion, and politics. "We cheer for the Senators, we pray for the Senators, and we hope that the Supreme Court does not declare that unconstitutional," LBJ said.

At his first game as president, the 1964 opener, U.S. senators in attendance were called back to the Capitol via stadium loudspeaker for a quorum call on the Civil Rights Bill. After the team dropped the game, 4–0, to the Los Angeles Angels, some joked that "the wrong senators were asked to leave the ballpark." The next year, LBJ was spotted eating four hot dogs and a bag of popcorn. Washington lost that one, too, 7–2, to the Red Sox, with all nine runs coming on home runs.

For Johnson, baseball was not a high priority. In 1966, when team officials came to the White House for the annual presentation of the season pass, LBJ met with them for about 30 seconds, and then allowed photographers just 30 seconds to take pictures. He then clapped his hands and said, "Let's go, we've got a lot of things to do." Facing the Vietnam War and other pressing issues, Johnson would miss the opener that year as well as the opener in 1968, his final year in office.

Richard Nixon was probably the most knowledgeable baseball fan to occupy the Oval Office. He also had some experience at throwing out the first pitch prior to becoming president—in 1959, as vice president, he pinch-hit for Eisenhower. Later that year, Nixon traveled to the Soviet Union for the famous "Kitchen Debate" with Soviet Premier Nikita Khrushchev. His trip coincided with a horrible Senators losing streak that reached a dozen games.

According to former Washington slugger Roy Sievers, a Nixon favorite, the vice president called the ballpark from Russia and said, "I want Lemon, Killebrew, Allison, and Sievers out at the airport when the plane lands."

"We were all there," Sievers recalls. "The first thing he said was, 'What in the hell is wrong with the Senators?' And I said, 'Mr. Vice President, we're just not hitting good, the pitching's not good.'

"He said, 'I tell you what, I'll be out the next night.' Usually, when he'd come out, we'd win the ballgame. But we lost." In fact, the Senators' streak hit 18 before they finally snapped it with a victory over the Cleveland Indians.

Years later, Nixon recalled how taxing it was to be a Senators fan. "You have to have been a real baseball fan to have been a fan of the Senators," Nixon said at gala luncheon at the Richard Nixon Presidential Library & Birthplace in 1992. "It was no easier to have been a fan of the Senators we had back then than of some of the senators we have in Washington today."

In the mid-1960s, Nixon was out of politics after losing the presidential race in 1960 and the California governor's race in 1962. His career could have taken a different path at that point: he was approached by baseball owners to become commissioner, and by the players' union to become its director, according to *Baseball: The President's Game*. Nixon, of course, went on to become president in 1969. Ironically, George W. Bush tried to gauge interest in becoming baseball commissioner when he was owner of the Texas Rangers, before settling on the White House in 2001.

Nixon made his presidential baseball debut in 1969, along with the team's new manager, Ted Williams, as the Senators lost, 8–4, to the New York Yankees. Sitting next to Nixon was another rookie, Bowie Kuhn, in his first year as baseball commissioner. Kuhn recalls telling Nixon about how Williams was trying to make Senators slugger Frank Howard a more disciplined hitter.

"So here comes Howard to bat, the first pitch bounces six feet in front of home plate, and he swings and misses," Kuhn says with a laugh. "And the president looked at me, and didn't say a word. His silence spoke volumes. We both laughed. He was a great baseball fan."

In July of that season, the president received the world champion Detroit Tigers at the White House, who were escorted by Congressman Gerald R. Ford of Michigan—the man who would replace Nixon after the Watergate scandal five years later.

"You know I have to be for Washington—do you mind?" he asked the Tigers. Referring to the Senators' 3–0 victory over Detroit the day before, Nixon quipped, "You don't mind passing the wealth around, do you?"

"Yes we do," one of the players laughingly replied.

That night, Nixon was at the ballpark to see the Senators win a second straight game against the Tigers, 7–3. It also marked the team's second consecutive victory with Nixon in attendance.

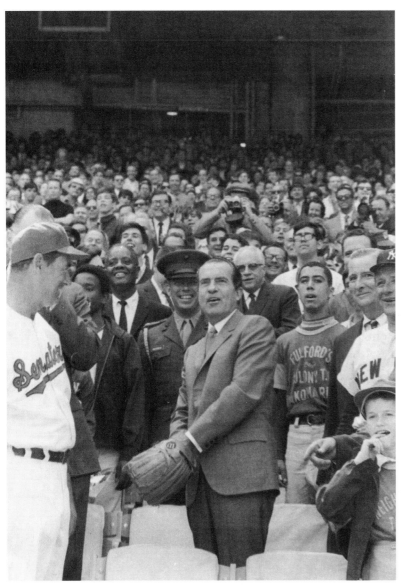

President Richard Nixon winds up as Ted Williams (left) looks on, in the Senators'
opening game with New York in 1969. Library of Congress

Nixon was such a huge fan that in 1972, he compiled an all-time All-Star team for the Associated Press. "I like the job I have now," he once said, "but if I had my life to live over again, I'd like to have ended up a sportswriter."

"Of all the presidents, Nixon was the most knowledgeable baseball fan," says Brotman, the former public address announcer. "At first, I told his administrative assistant, he must have really boned up, because he's talking to players about batting averages and earned run average. And the aide said, 'No, no, no, he didn't bone up. He really is a baseball fan. He follows it through the sports pages.'"

When the Senators were on the verge of moving to Texas in 1971, Nixon said it would be "heartbreaking," but he declined to get personally involved.

"This may have been practical politics by the president, who can count and is aware of Texas' 28 electoral votes compared to the District of Columbia's mere three," *Washington Post* sports editor Shirley Povich wrote in a requiem for the team. "But it was also pussyfooting, and entirely unlike the pronouncement in 1958 by then-Vice President Nixon that a Washington without major league baseball would be 'unthinkable.'"

Still, Nixon was working behind the scenes to get a team back. On October 13, 1971, he met with D.C. Mayor Walter E. Washington to discuss the prospects. In a tape-recorded conversation, previously unreported, Nixon mentions several candidates: "The White Sox is (sic) a possibility. Chicago really can't support two teams."

At another point, he asks about luring the Cleveland Indians. "Cleveland is not going to support them. They got that lousy lakefront stadium," the president says.

"And they haven't had any attendance," Washington says. The Indians were the only team that year to draw less than the Senators, pulling in 591,000 fans, compared to Washington's 655,000.

The president also tees off on the Senators' owner, Bob Short, who had been a chief fundraiser for Nixon's 1968 opponent, Hubert H. Humphrey.

"Short is a jerk," Nixon declares. "I sat behind him at games, and I can tell you—moaning and bitching all the time."

At the end of the meeting, Nixon makes an optimistic—and as history would prove inaccurate—prediction.

"I think that with Washington, the (bi)centennial coming up and everything, baseball will be back," he says. In that bicentennial year, 1976, the American League owners voted to expand outside the country, to Toronto, and to another Washington—Seattle.

Although Nixon told Mayor Washington that losing the Senators was "terrible," he was not above trying to capitalize on it politically. On September 22, 1971, the day after the American League voted to allow Short to move the team to Texas, White House press secretary Ron Ziegler told reporters that Nixon would now switch his allegiance to the California Angels, near his home of San Clemente, California.

That night, in another previously unreported taped conversation, Nixon called Robert H. Finch, a longtime Nixon loyalist.

"I want you to call (Angels owners) Bob Reynolds and Gene Autry and tell them that the president thinks this is a very significant thing," Nixon tells Finch. "For seventy-one years, presidents, oh, going back to William Howard Taft and all the rest, Theodore Roosevelt, have thrown out balls in Washington." (He was off by about 10 years and one president—Teddy Roosevelt never threw a ball out at a Senators game.)

"The president has in effect said, now, that with this change, that each president should throw out the ball in the park of his home team. Now what they have to do is change the American League schedule, so that the first game, you see, the way Washington always played the first game, will be in Anaheim Stadium, see? And I'll come out and throw out the ball, and I agree to do it, see?"

Maybe Nixon was cut out for baseball commissioner after all.

"It's really a big deal," Nixon says.

No argument from Finch. "I think it's great," he says.

But the plan was never put into motion. When the American League schedule came out, the Angels were slated to open on the road in Minnesota, although the game was cancelled because of a brief players strike.

After Washington lost the Senators, presidents would head north to Baltimore to throw out the first ball, but it didn't have the same pomp and circumstance of the capital openers. Kuhn, the former commissioner, remembers President Ronald Reagan's appearance in Baltimore in 1988, when Frank Robinson was the Orioles manager.

"After President Reagan threw out the ball, he said to me, 'I'd like to sit in the dugout,'" Kuhn says. "The president selected the home plate end of dugout, and that's where Robinson sat. So Robinson sat on the other side of the dugout. He did a slow burn, and glared at us on the other end of the dugout. It lasted two innings."

Seventeen years later, Robinson was in the dugout at RFK when the presidential tradition resumed in Washington with George W. Bush, a one-time owner of the Texas Rangers, the last team to play in Washington.

"I'm excited about the team," Bush told reporters. "I started paying attention to the lineups during spring training. I watch the pitching staff. I know that Livan Hernandez is pitching tonight. I'm watching carefully."

Bush saw Nationals pitcher Joey Eischen in the clubhouse before the game, and remembered that the Rangers had traded him for Oil Can Boyd.

"Eischen, right?" the president asked.

"Yes, sir," Eischen responded.

"Oil Can Boyd. Bad trade."

Unfortunately, Bush's appearance kept thousands of fans waiting outside the ballpark as the game began, where they were forced to stand in long lines to go through metal detectors. But the fans went home happy, as the Nationals won their first home game ever, defeating the Arizona Diamondbacks, 5–3, in front of a capacity crowd of 45,596.

Bush, the son of a former Yale first baseman, made sure he got some practice throws before the day of the game. The president had the opening pitch on his mind that afternoon, telling the American Society of Newspaper Editors: "I've got a decision to make. Do I go with the fastball or a slider?"

He went with the fastball, sending a high, hard one to Nationals catcher Brian Schneider, and bringing a sense of closure to the final Senators game ever played. Thirty-four years earlier, fans swarmed onto the field with two outs in the ninth inning, and the last out of the last game was never recorded. The man on the mound in the middle of that dark anti-celebration, Senators pitcher Joe Grzenda, pocketed the ball and kept it all these years in his home in Pennsylvania. As baseball returned to Washington in 2005, he handed the ball to Bush for the opening toss.

SIX

FUTILITY

SIX

FUTILITY

The Senators suffered a huge disappointment after winning the 1933 pennant. They finished 20 games under .500 in 1934, ending up in seventh place, 34 games behind the American League champion Detroit Tigers. That season signaled a fundamental shift in Washington's fortunes. The team would finish in the top half of the standings just four times from 1934 until it moved to Minnesota in 1961.

Washington began taking apart its championship team even before the 1934 season started, releasing future Hall-of-Fame outfielder Sam Rice in the off-season. At the age of 43, Rice had been a backup on the '33 team, but had helped contribute, batting .294 off the bench. It was Rice's 19th season in the big leagues, all in a Washington uniform.

"Sam, it is with deep regret that the time has come when your service with the Washington team is ended," owner Clark Griffith wrote to the player nicknamed Man O'War, "but I hope our personal friendship will carry on for all time."

Rice finished his career in 1934 with the Cleveland Indians, batting .293—a good season for most, but the lowest of Rice's 20-year career. He retired with a lifetime batting average of .322 and 351 stolen bases.

In August 1934, the Senators dumped pitcher Al Crowder, who had helped the 1933 team win the pennant with a staff-high 24 wins. Crowder, 35, had slumped badly in 1934, going 4–10 with a 6.79 ERA. The move was widely seen as the beginning of the breakup of the 1933 American League champions. But no one could have anticipated what was next.

The Boston Red Sox had a new wealthy owner, 31-year-old Tom Yawkey. Determined to turn the franchise around, he visited Griffith in his hotel room at the 1934 World Series and offered $250,000 for Washington player-manager Joe Cronin. That was an astonishingly high figure, presented in the midst of the Great Depression, and only 14 years after the Sox had sold Babe Ruth to the Yankees for $125,000.

Griffith had a quick reaction: "Tom, you had better leave."

After the series, Yawkey called the Old Fox at home and asked, "How about that deal?"

"To hell with you!" Griffith yelled, and hung up.

Griffith had good reason to be possessive of his star. He had nurtured Cronin from a punch-less .242 batter as a 21-year-old to one of the league's most dangerous hitters. In 1934, Cronin had knocked in 100 runs or more for the fifth straight time. He was the kind of manager Griffith liked, tough and determined. And Griffith could truly look upon his 28-year-old player-manager as a son: Cronin had recently married Griffith's niece and adopted daughter, Mildred Robertson.

Some muttered that Cronin had married into the manager's job for life. Such talk weighed on Griffith as he began to reconsider.

"I said to myself, 'You keep Cronin here and he will continue to be the subject of that son-in-law guff," Griffith wrote later. "Remember, Yawkey is a millionaire, with the sky the limit in his baseball operation. He could do things for Joe and Mildred you could never hope to approach."

Perhaps the Nats' owner was just rationalizing, although he conceded that family considerations weren't the only factors. Griffith recalled that the team had lost "a lot of money" in 1934, and that he owed a bank $124,000.

"I decided that, for the good of those two kids, and for the financial salvation of the Senators, I just had to let Cronin go to Boston."

But he demanded the Red Sox shortstop, Lyn Lary, and a five-year deal for his son-in-law at $30,000 a year. Lary lasted just 40 games in a Washington uniform, batting .194 in 1935 before the Senators shunted him off to the St. Louis Browns. Cronin played eleven seasons in Boston, seven as the team's regular shortstop, before finishing his playing career as a utility infielder.

In those seven seasons, Cronin hit .300 or better four times, drove in 100 runs or more three times, and even developed some power—hitting 17 or more home runs four times. In 13 seasons as Boston skipper, Cronin guided the team to nine winning records, including the 1946 pennant, the franchise's first since 1918. He was elected to the Hall of Fame in 1956.

Cronin wasn't the only family member Griffith unloaded. In 1941, he sold pitcher Joe Haynes, whose wife, Thelma Griffith, was another of Griffith's adopted daughters, to the Chicago White Sox. The Senators eventually reacquired Haynes, who became a coach and vice president of the team. Eleven years after trading Haynes, Griffith sold his own nephew, utility man Sherry Robertson, to the Philadelphia Athletics. Robertson, too, later returned to the flock, running the farm system.

By purchasing Cronin, the Red Sox were starting to make a habit of getting their managers from Washington. Boston's 1933 manager, Bucky Harris, had guided Washington to its first pennant nine years earlier. The Red Sox let him go to make room for Cronin, and in a bit of managerial musical chairs, Washington rehired its old manager for the 1934 season. Harris had been a success in his only year in Boston, leading the Red Sox to a fourth-place finish, a marked improvement over the team's seventh-place finish the year before.

Still only 38, Harris was no longer the "boy wonder" who had wowed the baseball world in the Roaring '20s. There was no magic in 1935, when the team improved by just ½ game over the previous season, finishing in sixth place, 9½ games under .500. Attendance slumped to 255,000, the worst since 1919. Second baseman Buddy Myer provided Senators fans with someone to cheer for, leading the league with a .349 batting average, and driving in 100 runs on just five homers.

That year, Griffith purchased pitcher Bobo Newsom from the St. Louis Browns for $50,000. In a sign of Washington's luck that season, a week later Newsom suffered a broken knee on a line drive in the third inning of a game, yet soldiered on to go the distance. "Tell the fans of Washington I'm sorry my bones ain't together," the colorful Newsom told reporters from the bed of his hotel room. "And tell them I'll be back there sooner than anybody says I will."

In 1936, Washington improbably jumped to fourth place with a record of 82–71. Newsom won 17 with 24 complete games, while Jimmie DeShong won 18. The season would turn out to be but a temporary reprieve for Washington fans, however. It was the Nats' only winning record from 1934 to 1942.

The Senators traded Newsom to the Red Sox in 1937, but he would return to Washington for four more stints. Griffith continued to try to retool the team that year by purchasing future Hall-of-Fame outfielder Al Simmons from the Detroit Tigers for $7,500. Simmons, 35, hit a disappointing .284 for the Senators, a drop of 48 points from the previous season in Detroit. He stepped it up in 1938, batting .302 with 21 home runs and 95 RBIs, but Griffith fined him $200 and released him at the end of the season after Simmons cursed out fans at Griffith Stadium.

"Simmons still is a good ball player, but he isn't satisfied with Washington nor does he fit in with my plans for a young team," Griffith said.

Despite the cascade of losing teams, Harris stuck around for eight seasons in his second tour with the Senators. But the manager didn't have much to work with, as Washington had a thin farm system.

Then, as now, there were complaints from "small-market teams" that bigger-market teams were threatening the competitive balance on which the sport depended—with the New York Yankees the poster boys for buying pennants.

Ironically, big-market teams were able to exploit their advantage by building up more expansive farm systems—the very tool that small-market teams use today to offset their financial disadvantage. The era of free agency was still a half-century away.

Washington was decidedly a small-market club. Griffith could afford only one farm team, compared to the 13 clubs owned by or affiliated with the Yankees. He demanded that the Yankees be forced to sell one of their two double-A teams.

"It's not the Yankees I'm against," he said in a 1940 *Saturday Evening Post* profile. "It's just the idea of preserving a monopoly by means of money. If we let those rich men run things the way that only they can afford to run them, what's going to become of baseball? You want John D. Rockefeller to come into baseball and win the pennant every year?"

Griffith was becoming an anachronism in the world of baseball owners—a former player who had mortgaged his ranch to buy into the team, competing against wealthy businessmen who did not depend on baseball for their livelihoods.

The Old Fox did shift his view on one major change to the game. In 1935, the Cincinnati Reds hosted the first major league night game, prompting Griffith to protest: "Baseball was meant to be played in God's own good sunshine."

But six years later, on May 28, 1941, the first night game at Griffith Stadium proved to be a real draw. Twenty-five thousand fans came out, five times the average crowd that year, to see former star Walter Johnson inaugurate the new era with a ceremonial first pitch. The stadium was dramatically thrust from darkness to light as the engineer flipped a switch to coincide with Johnson's toss. Game time was 8:30, an hour and a half later than today's starting time.

"Dignity went out the window as the gay and informal crowd shed its coats and rolled up its sleeves," the *Washington Post* reported, adding that the festivities "had all the fanfare of a Hollywood premiere." But the excitement and big crowd couldn't help the home team, which lost its 10th straight game that night.

The Senators continued to draw well under the stars, and Griffith became an enthusiastic supporter, successfully lobbying the league to let him hold more games without the benefit of God's own good sunshine. "When the National League instituted night competition, I hollered plenty," Griffith wrote years later. "I envisioned the ruination of the game in the major leagues. I regarded baseball after dark as strictly minor league stuff." But after the success of that first night game, he added, "I realized then that I had been wrong about the innovation." While night baseball may have energized Griffith in 1941, something else weighed heavily on his mind: the prospect of a last-place finish. In August of that year, the team slipped into the American League basement.

"You don't understand it," he told reporters before a loss to the Yankees at Griffith Stadium. "But right now I'm a heap more jittery than I'd be if we were fighting for a first-division place. It's been thirty years since I came here, and in all that time we never finished in the cellar. I just don't want to finish last."

The loss to New York dropped Washington 10½ games under .500. But the Senators actually played over .500 the rest of the way, ending in sixth and averting the last-place finish Griffith so dreaded. Shortstop Cecil Travis was the exception to the team's mediocrity, batting .359, two points ahead of MVP Joe DiMaggio, who set the single-season record that season by hitting in 56 consecutive games. Travis was second only to Ted Williams, whose .406 batting average marked the last time an everyday player hit .400 or more.

The next year, 1942, Washington dropped to seventh place, and Harris quit as manager. The skipper who won two pennants in his first run with Washington had but one winning season in eight years this time around.

Once again, Griffith turned to an ex-Senators player to manage the team, this time Ossie Bluege, who had been the third baseman on the pennant-winning teams of 1924, 1925, and 1933.

Under Bluege's leadership, the Senators in 1943 posted their best record since their last pennant. Washington jumped to second place with an 84–69 record, 13½ games behind the first-place Yankees. Starting pitcher Early Wynn went 18–12 with a 2.91 ERA, while rookie Milo Candini won 11 games with a 2.49 ERA. The strong pitching helped overcome a lackluster offense that hit just .254 as a team. The Senators drew 575,000 fans, their highest total since 1930.

But the team sank back to bottom the next year, as Washington lost several key players to the military during World War II. Among those serving in the '44 season were first baseman Mickey Vernon, second baseman Gerry Priddy, and pitcher Ray Scarborough. Washington finished last with a .416 winning percentage, 25 games behind the St. Louis Browns, who won their only pennant that year. It was the first time a Senators team under Griffith had come in last place, and the first for the franchise in 35 years. Griffith was so desperate for players that he signed Eddie Boland, who had been playing for the New York City Sanitation Department team. Boland didn't do too bad, actually, hitting .271 in 19 games.

In 1945, for the third year in a row, Washington did a complete somersault in the standings. This time they would give their fans a season to remember—the Senators' last real pennant race.

Washington competed with a most unusual pitching staff. Four of the five starting pitchers—Roger Wolff, Dutch Leonard, Mickey Haefner, and Johnny Niggeling—were knuckleballers. This quartet had hitters tied up in knots, pitching 60 complete games among them and helping the Senators to a league-best 2.92 ERA. Wolff (20–10, 2.12 ERA) and Leonard (17–12, 2.13 ERA) paced the staff, while the rotation's sole non-knuckleballer, a five-foot, seven-inch native of Lucca, Italy, named Marino Pieretti, won 14 games.

On offense, Washington made up for a lack of punch with speed on the base paths. The Senators hit just 27 home runs that year, and incredibly, just one at home—an inside-the-parker by first baseman Joe Kuhel. But Washington hit a league-high 63 triples, led by Kuhel's 13. Paced by outfielder George Case and second baseman George Myatt, who swiped 30 bases each, the Senators also led the league in stolen bases. Washington got a lift in late June when outfielder Buddy Lewis returned from the Pacific Theater, where he had been flying cargo planes over the Himalayas. Lewis hit .333 with seven triples in 70 games.

The most colorful player on the team, however, was outfielder Bingo Binks. The 28-year-old rookie had spent the first two years of the war working as a machinist in a war-materials factory. Although a talented athlete with great defensive skills, he hadn't mastered the game's fundamentals, infuriating his manager, Bluege. Because he was deaf in one ear, Binks had been disqualified from serving in the military

"Bluege would chew him out from time to time, and Binks would say, 'I haven't heard one word you said,'" wrote Bill Gilbert, who served as the team's batboy that spring. "He would drive this old-school manager up the wall."

A turning point for the Senators came in mid-summer. Entering August, Washington was just four games over .500, in fourth place. The Nats then started a string of five doubleheaders in five days against the Philadelphia Athletics and Boston Red Sox at Griffith Stadium. Washington won 9 of the 10 games, catapulting into second place with a 54–42 record, hot on the heels of the first-place Detroit Tigers.

The city buzzed that year over the pennant race, and the ballpark was often filled with uniformed men from all branches of the military in what would be the final year of World War II.

"You would see this sea of colors of military uniforms in the stands: the Army khakis, the Navy white uniforms, the Marine green," says Gilbert. "When a hitter hit a ball into the stands, the fan who caught it always threw it back, because they knew that those balls would go to the military bases for the GIs playing baseball. And if you started to stick it in your pocket, you'd get booed right out of the ballpark."

Washington Senator Buddy Lewis was one of many of major league baseball's players to have forsaken the game to serve their country during World War II. Here he is shown with fellow air cadets at Kelly Air Force Field in April 1942. Rucker Archive

Washington and Detroit battled it out the rest of the way, but because of a scheduling quirk, the Senators would finish their season a week before the Tigers. Griffith rented out his stadium to the Washington Redskins every year, and the Senators ended their schedule early in 1945 to allow the football team to play its home opener on September 30. That's one reason the Nats had played so many doubleheaders back in August.

So Washington entered a season-ending three-game series on September 22 against the Athletics in Philadelphia 1½ games behind the Tigers. The Senators won the first game, 2–0, then suited up for a doubleheader the next day, knowing they needed a sweep to pull even with the Tigers. But in this improbable season, a sunny break in the afternoon cast a cloud on the Senators' pennant chances.

The first game of the doubleheader went into extra innings, and in the bottom of the 12th with two outs, Philadelphia's Ernie Kish lofted a fly ball to center field. The sun had just come out, and Binks, Washington's center fielder, had forgotten his sunglasses. Losing the ball in the sun, Binks couldn't make the catch, and Kish wound up with a double. Kish scored the winning run on a single, driving a dagger into the Nationals' pennant chances.

The Senators came back to win the second game, 4–3, but found themselves a game out of first—and no games left to play. Now all they could do was hope the Tigers would lose three of their remaining games. That would result in a tie, and a one-game playoff to decide the pennant winner.

The Tigers split their first two games, giving Washington fans hope. Now the Senators needed the defending American League champions, the St. Louis Browns, to sweep a season-ending doubleheader against the Tigers on a rainy day in St. Louis. In the first game, the Browns led 3–2 after eight innings, but in the top of the ninth, the Tigers loaded the bases with one out. Up came their star, Hank Greenberg, who had returned from the Army in June. Hammerin' Hank parked one into the left-field bleachers, giving Detroit a 6–3 lead. The Tigers held St. Louis scoreless in the bottom of the ninth, clinching the pennant, and ending Washington's season. Detroit would go on to win the World Series against the Chicago Cubs.

The Senators, meanwhile, finished 10 games over .500, their best record since the 1933 season. It was a mark they would never match again.

The next year was a financial success but disappointing on the field. The Senators drew a franchise record 1,027,000 people to Griffith Stadium in 1946, the only time they broke the one-million mark, as fans came out in hopes of another pennant race. But this time, Washington dropped to fourth place, finishing with a 76–78 record, 28 games out of first. Although Vernon topped the league with a .353 batting average and 51 doubles, the team suffered from substandard pitching and defense. The Senators were the worst fielding team in the league and had the third-worst ERA.

On December 10 of that year, after a nine-month illness, Walter Johnson died from a brain tumor at the age of 59. Among those keeping vigil at Johnson's bedside was Clark Griffith. Thousands came to Johnson's memorial service at the Washington National Cathedral. Former teammates served as pallbearers, along with former Giants pitcher Jack Bentley, whom Johnson had defeated in the seventh game of the 1924 World Series.

The 1946 season started a long slide for the Senators. In 1947, the team dropped to seventh place with a .416 winning percentage, 33 games behind the first-place Yankees, piloted by former Nats manager Bucky Harris. For the second year in a row, the American League champions were managed by a former Senators skipper; Joe Cronin had guided the Red Sox to the flag in 1946.

Vernon, the '46 batting champion, dropped nearly 100 points in 1947, finishing with a .265 average. The Senators hit a woeful .241 as a team, with no regular over .280. After the season, Griffith relieved Bluege as manager, making him director of the Senators' farm system.

Of course, Griffith hired a former player to replace Bluege—this time, the team's old first baseman, Joe Kuhel. Although Kuhel belonged to the American Society of Magicians, he could work no magic on this team. The 1948 Nats lost 18 straight games in September en route to another seventh-place finish, and a .366 winning percentage. Vernon, just two years after winning the batting title, bottomed out at .242. After the season, Griffith traded him, along with pitcher Early Wynn, to Cleveland for first baseman Eddie Robinson and two pitchers. In shipping off Wynn, Washington had dealt a future Hall-of-Famer.

In 1949, the Senators started out 1–7, then shocked the baseball world by winning nine straight games on a road trip to improve to 12–11. The Senators dropped the last game of the trip to fall to .500, but that was good enough for their overly optimistic fans. Although it was only May, thousands gathered at Union Station to welcome the "Wondrous Nats" back to Washington as heroes. The players were treated to a motorcade down Pennsylvania Avenue, and city commissioners and U.S. senators were predicting a pennant. "We knew all along on the Hill that we had the best team in the American League," said Senator Millard Tydings, a Maryland Democrat. Fans even called the ballpark inquiring about reserving World Series tickets.

By early June, the surprising Nats were 25–20. But as baseball fans relearn every year, it's a long season. The team tanked after its strong start, ending up not as the best team in the league but the worst. In fact, Washington's 50–104 record (.325 percentage) was its worst since 1909. Three starters posted ERAs over 5.00—Paul Calvert (6–17, 5.43), Mickey Harris (2–12, 5.16), and Dick Weik (3–12, 5.38).

By the end of the season, it was obvious to everyone—including Kuhel—that the manager would be fired. "I'll probably be canned at the end of the season and I'm not griping," he was quoted as saying. "That's baseball. But in my defense, I'd like to say this: You can't make chicken salad out of chicken feathers." Turns out he probably said something more colorful than "feathers."

After two seasons, Kuhel was out as manager. For his replacement, Griffith turned to his old standby—Bucky Harris—for his third tour of duty with the team. Harris had led the Yankees to a pennant in 1947 but was fired after the team slipped to third place in 1948. He was managing in the minors when Griffith asked him to return to Washington. The Nats owner gave Harris, 52, a three-year contract, breaking with the team's tradition of hiring managers for just one year at a time.

In the off-season, when Griffith turned 80, he encountered the only serious challenge to his control of the team. Since purchasing a controlling interest of the Senators after the 1919 season with wealthy Philadelphia exporter William Richardson, Griffith had enjoyed a free rein with the team. So he never felt the need to acquire a controlling interest on his own, knowing that Richardson would always back his decisions. Between the two of them, they held about 80 percent of the team's stock.

But after the Richardson estate put the 40 percent ownership stake up for sale, 31-year-old investor John J. Jachym purchased it for $550,000 on behalf of an investment syndicate. Although Jachym stressed that he had no designs on taking over the place, he also made it clear that he was not going to be a passive investor. He had baseball experience as a scout for the St. Louis Cardinals and a minor league baseball owner. For his part, Griffith had no interest in sharing ownership responsibilities with the youngster.

The Old Fox owned about 40 percent of the team's stock and couldn't freeze Jachym out on his own. So he enlisted other investors in the team to keep Jachym at bay—declining the upstart partner a seat on the board of directors, and even refusing to give him an office at the ballpark. Jachym irritated Griffith with such grandiose proposals as a Triple-A team, season ticket sales, a modern scoreboard, and a public relations director—all elements, of course, of today's teams.

"For his $550,000, Johnny got a 10-cent brush off," wrote *Washington Star* columnist Francis Stann.

Within six months, Jachym sold out his 40 percent share to H. Gabriel Murphy. "I had the rug pulled out from under me," Jachym said. At least he made an $85,000 profit on the sale.

Murphy was in the mold of William Richardson—a pliant partner. "I bought into the Washington club strictly as an investor," Murphy said. "I have no recommendations to make. Mr. Griffith is the boss and I'll go along with him in every way. I'm not a baseball man; Mr. Griffith is the best."

Delighted with the switch, Griffith made Gabriel a vice president. "Now we can go ahead without any worries," Griffith said. Murphy made sure of that when he agreed to sell Griffith enough of his own stock to give the Old Fox controlling ownership. Ironically, after Griffith's death five years later, Murphy would become a steely adversary to Clark Griffith's successor, Calvin Griffith, battling the new owner's plans to move the team out of Washington.

Meanwhile, Bucky Harris brought a modicum of baseball success to the Senators in 1950—at least by the team's low standards. Washington jumped to fifth place, but still finished 10 games under .500, and 31 games out of first place. The team's young third baseman, Eddie Yost, was starting to come into his own. Just 23, Yost hit .295 and scored 114 runs. Yost, who would become known as "The Walking Man," led the league with 141 walks, and finished second with an on-base percentage of .440.

On May 31, the Senators traded their first baseman, Eddie Robinson, who had gotten off to a slow start, and two weeks later reacquired Vernon to take his place. Vernon, who was hitting just .190 with the Indians through the first two months of the season, rediscovered his stroke with the Nats, batting .306 the rest of the way.

Although Washington improved by 17 games in 1950, their fans were not returning. The Senators drew just under 700,000, their fourth straight season of dwindling attendance. That trend continued, for the most part, throughout the 1950s.

The Senators slumped to seventh place in 1951, but Harris managed to squeeze a winning season out of them in 1952—barely. The team finished 78–76, good for fifth place, in what would be its last winning season in Washington. The Nats were even within striking distance of first place most of the year. In late August, they were 7½ games off the pace, but finished 17 games behind the pennant-winning Yankees. Griffith rewarded Harris with a new two-year contract as manager.

Washington made up for an anemic offense that year with outstanding starting pitching. Nats batters hit a league-worst .239, but three starting pitchers posted ERAs under 3.00—Bob Porterfield (2.72), Connie Marrero (2.88), and Spec Shea (2.93). Plagued by poor run support, this trio combined for only 35 victories.

Marrero, just five feet seven inches tall, was one of the colorful Cuban players signed by super scout Joe Cambria. He was coy about his age, although baseball records indicate he was 41 years old that season. "When baseball writers attempted to wheedle from Marrero his exact age," Shirley Povich wrote in *The Washington Senators*, "he merely grinned and pointed awkwardly to the number on his baseball shirt which read '22.'" Marrero completed 16 of his 22 starts that year and finished with an 11–8 record.

The Senators had an almost identical record the next season, 1953, 76–76, again good for fifth place. This time, the hitting and pitching were more evenly matched, allowing Porterfield to lead the league with 22 wins despite his ERA increasing by more than a half-run to 3.35. He also led the league in shutouts (nine) and complete games (24).

Washington had some hitting stars as well. Vernon led the league with a .337 batting average and 43 doubles, and was second in both RBIs (115) and triples (11). A rejuvenated Washington offense hit a respectable .263 that year.

Although it played some exciting baseball, Washington's attendance went into a freefall that year. The team drew just 596,000 fans, a drop-off of more than 100,000 from the previous year, and its lowest total since 1944.

In 1954, the Senators had new competition in the region. The woeful St. Louis Browns had moved to Baltimore to become the Orioles. After getting some financial concessions, Griffith agreed to waive his territorial rights to the region, a gesture which was not reciprocated by the Orioles years later, when they fought to keep a team out of Washington.

For the Senators, sharing a regional fan base was hardly the only problem the Browns' move posed. Washington also lost a fellow bottom-dweller in the American League. The Browns had been one of the worst teams for decades. As recently as 1951, only a last-place finish by St. Louis helped the Senators avoid the cellar; Washington finished seventh that year. The Senators might have won only three pennants, but the Browns had managed just one—and that was in 1944, when major league teams were stocked with inferior players filling in for regulars fighting in World War II.

The relationship between these two teams changed almost immediately. The Orioles finished behind the Nats in their first year in Baltimore, but drew around a million fans—double Washington's attendance, which had tumbled to

Harmon Killebrew (left) joined the Senators in 1954. Here he is welcomed to the team by Bucky Harris (center) and player Bob Porterfield (right). Rucker Archive

503,000. At one home game, the Senators played in front of just 460 fans. These franchises were going in opposite directions, both at the turnstiles and on the field. The Orioles would never finish lower than the original Senators again.

Washington did pull one fast one on its new neighbor. Before the 1954 season, the Senators traded outfielder Gil Coan to Baltimore for outfielder–first baseman Roy Sievers. Coan was out of baseball by 1956, while Sievers emerged as one of the top sluggers in the American League. The Senators also made another shrewd move by purchasing from the Cleveland Indians Jim Lemon, who would also develop into a bona fide slugger. But the 1954 season was a disappointment for the Senators. After two decent years, Washington dropped into sixth place, 11 games under .500.

The Senators fired Harris after the season and replaced him with former Brooklyn Dodgers manager Chuck Dressen. It was Griffith's last managerial move, and it marked the first time he chose someone who hadn't been a Senators player. Harris, who had managed the Nats for 18 years in three different stints, took the manager's job in Detroit.

Dressen was coming off two straight pennant-winning Dodgers teams in 1952 and 1953, but he could not reverse the Nats' slide. The 1955 Senators finished in last place with a .344 winning percentage. Attendance tanked to a league-worst 425,000, marking the first time since 1917 that Washington had been outdrawn by every other American League team. The average Nats crowd in 1955 was just over 5,500.

That season also saw the end of an era in Washington. On October 27, 1955, Griffith died at the age of 85. The Old Fox had been with the team, as manager and then owner, for 33 years.

Thousands came to his funeral, including scores of players, managers, and executives from across baseball. Among them were Griffith's two "boy wonder" player-managers, Bucky Harris and Joe Cronin, now middle-aged men of 58 and 49, respectively. Harris and Cronin had accounted for all three of Washington's pennants between them, the last one coming 22 years earlier.

"Mr. Griffith was a man of the Old West," recalls Bob Wolff, the team's first television announcer. "He believed in loyalty and trust. At noon, he cleared everyone out of his office except his family. They'd all eat lunch at a big long table. They all worked at the ballpark, or played for him."

Then after the game, Griffith would sit in his office by himself, listening to *The Lone Ranger* on the radio, Wolff says, and in later years, watching it on television after day games. Widow, Addie Griffith, recalled how her husband had put everything into the team.

"He had some hard times, believe me," she told the *Washington Post* in 1956. "It was a struggle. People talk about all the money he had. He never had any money to spend. We never went abroad or took airplane trips. It was always throwing money into the club—every cent we ever had. Clark wasn't rich like the Comiskeys and the Macks."

With his death, Griffith's nephew and adopted son, Calvin Griffith, who had been serving as team president, took control of the team. The Senators were in poor financial straits, Calvin Griffith told biographer Jon Kerr years later. "When I took the club over in 1955 I think we had $25,000 in the treasury."

Within one month, the young Griffith traded away his star first baseman, Vernon, in a nine-player deal with the Red Sox. Washington didn't receive any impact players in the deal.

Calvin Griffith soon entertained more consequential offers—to move the team out of Washington. In October 1956, after another disastrous year in which the Senators finished seventh and drew just 432,000 fans, Griffith told reporters that he was considering moving the team to either Los Angeles or San Francisco. At the time, there was no major league baseball on the West Coast.

Gabriel Murphy, Clark Griffith's accommodating partner, now turned on Calvin Griffith. Murphy, who owned 40 percent of the team's stock, threatened to sue Griffith to prevent a move.

"I am shocked and saddened to learn that those who succeeded to Mr. Griffith's position would try to erase his efforts within fifty-eight days after the Washington baseball fans erected a monument to his memory," Murphy said. "The Senators must remain in Washington. I feel, as others in baseball, that our club is not merely a local representative. This is a national baseball team. It belongs to the nation as does the city itself."

In the end, the team's board of directors considered bids from four cities—Los Angeles, San Francisco, Minneapolis, and Louisville—before deciding to stay put. "We're happy to remain here and I hope we stay here the rest of our lives," Griffith said.

Addie Griffith called the news wonderful. "Clark loved this city and I know he never would have left Washington," she said. Clark Griffith had opposed any discussion of moving the team.

But Murphy said the damage had been done. "The attempt to move the franchise to the West Coast seriously impaired the value of the club's most priceless asset—the wholehearted support and confidence of the Washington fans," he said in announcing he was quitting his salaried job of board treasurer and director in early 1957, while retaining his stock in the team.

Meanwhile, Griffith was trying to assure Washington fans the team would stay—for good. In a January 15, 1957, piece in the *Washington Post*, Griffith wrote: "This is my home. I intend that it shall remain my home for the rest of my life. As long as I have any say in the matter and I expect that I shall for a long, long time, the Washington Senators will stay here too. Next year. The year after. Forever."

Griffith later blamed those famous last words on the team's overeager public relations man, who had ghostwritten the piece for him.

The Senators' attendance was truly woeful. Thirteen of the sport's 16 baseball teams drew more in 1956 than Washington drew in 1955 and 1956 *combined*. In 1957, the team dropped back into last place, and its attendance remained last in the league—457,000. Griffith fired Dressen after a 4–16 start and replaced him with Cookie Lavagetto.

There was a bright spot on that dreadful Washington team—the performance of Roy Sievers. The Senators' slugger hit .301 and led the league in both home runs (42) and RBIs (114). He also tied an American League record by hitting six home runs in six games. His record-tying home run came in the 17th inning, on his eighth at bat of the day, giving Washington a 4–3 victory over the Detroit Tigers.

"The next day, the wind's blowing out, and I was hoping to break the record," Sievers recalls. "I hit four pop flies."

After the season, Sievers went into Calvin Griffith's office and asked for a 100 percent raise. Griffith balked, Sievers recalls, but did wind up giving him a decent salary. Sievers' 1957 paycheck of $36,000 was the highest ever for a Senator.

"So I come back the next year, after hitting 39 home runs, driving in 108 runs, and batting .295," Sievers says. "He wanted to cut me $10,000!"

After the 1957 season, the two California cities that had sought out the Senators the year before lured the National League's two New York teams, the Dodgers and Giants, to the West Coast. At a board meeting in January 1958, Griffith said he hoped to keep the Senators in Washington as long as he lived. Asked by a stockholder, "Do you assure the stockholders the club will remain here?" Griffith said, "Yes."

But six months later, Griffith was claiming that he was being pushed to move the team by four owners who served on the American League's relocation committee. "Some clubs are raising hell with us," Griffith said on the eve of a league owners' meeting. "They're sick and tired of playing to small crowds" in Washington. Minneapolis, Houston, and Toronto expressed interest in the Senators.

Griffith's claim was refuted by Yankees owner Del Webb, chairman of the American League relocation committee. "This hits me cold," Webb told the *Post*. "Nobody ever indicated that the Washington club wanted to move or was being forced to move."

At the owners' meeting, Griffith decided not to ask permission to relocate the team after getting resistance from fellow owners, who were concerned about the timing, as Congress was considering legislation to revoke baseball's coveted antitrust exemption. Senator J. Glenn Beall, a Maryland Republican, sent a telegram to American League President Will Harridge, warning that it would be "unthinkable" for baseball to desert the nation's capital.

Just a week later, however, Griffith acknowledged in testimony before a Senate subcommittee that he still might move the team. "We want to stay in Washington as long as humanly possible," Griffith said. "Baseball is a business. If we don't get enough fans, we're going to have to find out if we can carry on. We can't leave the franchise to stay here and rot."

It was doing just that. In 1958, the team once again finished last in both the standings and attendance, drawing just 475,000 fans. The team finished eighth again in 1959, but attendance improved as the team offered fans a couple of new young sluggers. One was 24-year-old Bob Allison, who hit 30 home runs. The other was 22-year-old Harmon Killebrew, who shared the league lead in home runs with 42.

Killebrew became a Washington Senator because of a U.S. senator. Five years earlier, Clark Griffith's friend, Senator Herman Welker of Idaho, told the Nats' owner about a teenager from his hometown of Payette, Idaho, who was worth checking out. Griffith sent Ossie Bluege to scout the 17-year-old Killebrew, who went 12-for-12 in a semipro game. Bluege quickly signed the youngster.

Fueled by Killebrew, Allison, and Lemon, who hit 33 home runs that year, the suddenly explosive Senators increased their attendance by 130,000 that 1959 season to 615,000. Still, Calvin Griffith was again entertaining offers to move the team to Minneapolis, saying he needed at least 700,000 fans.

"What more does Mr. Griffith expect of fans who have seen the Senators end up in last place for three seasons in a row and in the second division for the past thirteen seasons?" asked the *Washington Star* in an October 6, 1959, editorial.

When it became clear again that he didn't have the votes among his fellow American League owners to approve a relocation after the season, Griffith announced the team would not move.

Murphy rhetorically—and prophetically—asked what good that statement was. "What happens next year?" he said. "Do we go into orbit again in 1960?"

In a word—yes.

In October, 1960, Griffith finally won league permission to move the team, coupled with expansion that would put new teams in Washington and Los Angeles. The American League fast-tracked the expansion for the 1961 season to beat the National League to the punch. The senior circuit had already announced new teams in Houston and New York for 1962.

Ironically, in their last year in Washington, the Senators had their best season in seven years, finishing in fifth place. Attendance increased to 743,000, the highest since 1949.

"I regret leaving Washington, but I just couldn't turn down the Minneapolis deal," Griffith said. "I think we'll draw 1.3 million our first year there and we'll average more per head than we did at Washington." Griffith wasn't too far off. In their first year in Minneapolis, the newly-named Twins drew 1.26 million fans—more than they drew in any year in Washington.

The Twins developed into a successful franchise. They won the pennant in 1965 and back-to-back division titles in 1969 and 1970. In 1987, the Twins won the World Series, the franchise's first in more than 60 years, dating back to the 1924 Senators. But a decade after the team's second championship in 1991, Major League Baseball tried to extinguish the team, which had been a charter member of the American League, born in Washington a century earlier. After the 2001 World Series, MLB targeted the Twins and the Montreal Expos for elimination.

In fighting off the plan, the state of Minnesota, which had lured away Washington's first team, paved the way for baseball's return to the nation's capital. The state-chartered Metropolitan Sports Facilities Commission won an injunction forcing the Twins to play in the Metrodome the following season. Baseball couldn't eliminate just one team, because that would screw up scheduling. So the Expos glommed on to the Twins' lifeline.

As part of a collective bargaining agreement reached a year later, baseball owners pledged not to eliminate any teams through 2006. That meant the only way to get rid of the problem child Expos was to move them. Had the Twins gone under, there would have been no Expos to move to Washington. In a strange way, Washington owes its new team to the state that took its old team away.

SEVEN

A DOOMED REBIRTH:
THE EXPANSION SENATORS

A DOOMED REBIRTH: THE EXPANSION SENATORS

There was something unfair about Washington having to start all over again with an expansion team in 1961. After all, the American League wasn't "expanding" to D.C. at all; the nation's capital had been a charter member of the league, dating back to 1901. It was Minneapolis that was the real expansion city, but it was not forced to pay its dues by starting from scratch. Instead, Minnesota received an up-and-coming Senators team from Washington.

The owners of the Cleveland Indians and Detroit Tigers argued that Calvin Griffith should have had to begin with an expansion team in Minnesota, and leave his players behind in Washington. But those owners were voted down six-to-two, so Washington got tagged with the new team. This was no semantic point. The old Senators were on the verge of success after seven straight losing seasons, thanks to rising stars such as Harmon Killebrew, Bob Allison, and Camilo Pascual. By 1965, the Twins would be American League pennant winners, something they hadn't achieved in their last 27 years in Washington.

"Like the San Francisco earthquake of 1908 which leveled a once-booming city, the New Nats must start from the bottom," *Washington Post* sportswriter Bob Addie wrote in a 1961 preview.

The new Senators and the other expansion team, the Los Angeles Angels, would be stocked with rejects from other American League teams during the expansion draft. Still, many Senators fans were glad to be rid of Calvin Griffith, and looked forward to a fresh start.

"The attitude of the local fans was, the old man, Clark Griffith was cheap—he had to be in order to survive. Calvin is cut from the same cloth. Cheap bastard. Let 'em go, we'll get another team," recalls Phil Hochberg, a lifelong Senators fan who become public address announcer for the new Senators.

The American League turned to a Washington bureaucrat to run the Washington Senators—Lt. Gen. Elwood R. (Pete) Quesada, the head of the Federal Aviation Administration. Quesada gave up his $20,000-a-year government salary to head up the ownership group. His family went back several generations in Washington, and there was (and still is) a Quesada Street in Northwest Washington, a few blocks west of Rock Creek Park.

Quesada beat out two competing ownership bids—one by New York financier John J. Bergen and the other by Washington lawyer Edward Bennett Williams, who listed Joe DiMaggio as a partner. In the early balloting, the Quesada and Williams bids each had the votes of three American League owners, with Bergen getting the support of the other two owners. The tie was broken, ironically, by the man who was deserting Washington—Calvin Griffith. He switched his vote from Williams to Quesada.

In an editorial, the *Washington Post* applauded the fact that the team would be owned by local investors, adding, "It was of the utmost importance that the Washington franchise be regarded as a long-term investment rather than as a speculative splurge." Unfortunately, the expansion Senators would have neither ownership stability, nor, at the end, a local owner—both factors that led to the team's move a decade later.

There was some uncertainty about whether the American League could actually get the new teams up and running for the next season. Baseball Commissioner Ford Frick, calling the American League expansion "hasty and impetuous," told the *Post*, "I believe in expansion. I always have. But I'd hate to see some town ruined by hasty action. There are many, many details to be discussed before a ball club can be put together."

But Congress soon made it clear that any delay in Washington's new team would be unacceptable. "Capitol Hill will not countenance any absence of major league baseball in Washington in 1961," said House Judiciary Committee Chairman Emanuel Celler, a New York Democrat. "The nation's capital shall not be looted of its franchise even for one season."

Quesada quickly named former Senators star first baseman Mickey Vernon as manager. Ed Doherty took the reigns as general manager and made a bold, and as it turned out, wildly inaccurate prediction: "With good trading and proper selection of players, we'll be a contending team in two or three years."

In the first-ever expansion draft on December 14, 1960, the new Senators chose 28 players at $75,000 each. The first player selected, Yankees pitcher Bobby Shantz, never suited up for the Senators. Washington traded him two days later to the Pittsburgh Pirates for pitcher Bernie Daniels and infielders Harry Bright and R. C. Stevens.

The trade paid early dividends for the newborn Senators. Daniels became Washington's only winning pitcher that first season, going 12–11 with a 3.44 ERA. Bright wasn't much of a factor that first season, but in 1962, he tied for the team lead in home runs with 17, batting .273.

The Angels and Senators picked players in four categories—pitchers, catchers, infielders, and outfielders. Washington's first infield pick was Detroit shortstop Coot Veal, who played a less-than-stellar season in his only year with in D.C., hitting .202 with just eight RBIs in 69 games. He was also thrown out eight times in nine stolen base attempts.

Washington chose as its first outfielder Boston's Willie Tasby, who hit .251 with 17 home runs and a team-high 63 RBIs in his first year with the team, and Kansas City's Dutch Dotterer as its first catcher, but Dotterer lost the starting job to Gene Green.

"A lot of things will be by trial and error," Vernon said before the '61 season. "There have been clubs which were new to their managers. But we have a situation here where neither is familiar with the other. . . . This is a completely new experience for everybody."

Spring training is the time of hope for all baseball teams, but it was especially promising for Washington's new team. The Senators had the best record in Florida's Grapefruit League, and broke camp with optimism for their first season. Sharing that optimism, hundreds of fans lined up before 7 a.m. the morning opening-day tickets went on sale.

"It was the most remarkable sales in the forty-two years I have been selling tickets for the ball team," tickets director Johnny Morrissey said. "Usually the fans hold off until the day of the game to buy those."

Two weeks later, April 10, 1961, was a day of both firsts and lasts. It was the first game of the new Washington Senators, but the last opener at Griffith Stadium, which was to be replaced the next season by D.C. Stadium (later renamed RFK). Unfortunately, the enthusiasm of a new beginning, 26,725 fans, and new President John F. Kennedy's strong first pitch couldn't get the team over the hump, as Washington fell, 4–3, to the Chicago White Sox. Former Senator Roy Sievers drove in the winning run with a sacrifice fly in the eighth inning.

But the team did win an important symbolic game a few weeks later. On May 26, the old Senators, now the Minnesota Twins, returned for the first time to Griffith Stadium to take on their successors. The new Senators beat the old ones, 4–3, behind the pitching of Joe McClain. Washington won the next two games, 14–4 and 6–4, to sweep the three-game series and make the catharsis complete.

It was a proud moment for the new franchise, which was still a tenant of Calvin Griffith in the old ballpark. Nearly 19,000 fans came out for the Sunday finale, a good showing for those days, and the third-best crowd in baseball that day. The sweep catapulted the Senators into fifth place in the 10-team league, and dumped the Twins into seventh place.

Washington won its next game against the Angels to climb up to .500 for the first time since the second game of the season. After a slow start, the Senators had gone 17–11 in May, surprising most experts, who had picked them for the bottom of the barrel. The Senators continued to play decent ball for the next couple of weeks, and at the 60-game mark their record stood at 30–30, quite respectable for a first-year team.

In mid-June, a trip north to Boston quickly turned the Senators' season south. The Red Sox rallied from a 6–0 deficit to beat the Senators 14–9 in the opener, and came back from 5–1 the next day for a 6–5 victory. The Sox must have felt they were on to something. In the first game of a Sunday doubleheader the next day, they waited until the ninth inning to make their move, rallying for eight runs with two outs to pull out a 13–12 victory. Thirteen proved an equally unlucky number in the nightcap, as Washington lost, 6–5, in 13 innings.

"You wouldn't believe it if you hadn't seen it, would you?" Vernon said.

Washington came home to play the Tigers in a three-game series, but home-cooking didn't help the Senators, who were swept again. Then they lost four more in Chicago to the White Sox. Now Washington had lost 10 in a row and had dropped like a rock to 30–40.

That spell couldn't begin to prepare D.C. fans for what would come later in the season. On September 1, the team lost its 14th straight game, leaving 11 men on base in a 3–2 decision to the White Sox. Washington snapped the streak the same day, winning the second game of a doubleheader, but it was just a temporary reprieve. The Senators lost another 10 in a row, punctuated by a doubleheader sweep by the Orioles in Baltimore. Over a 25-game period, Washington won just once—good for an .040 winning percentage.

When Washington suited up for the final game ever at Griffith Stadium, who better to see off the old ballpark than the Minnesota Twins? A victory over the ex-Senators would give the new Senators something to cherish from their first season. But the early-season Senators magic had vanished. They lost to the Twins, 6–3.

Not many people saw it. Just 1,498 fans showed up, the smallest crowd of the season. In the Washington dugout was 85-year-old Nick Altrock, who had joined the Washington Nationals as a pitcher back in 1912. Evangelist Elder Lightfoot Solomon Michaux of the neighboring Temple of Freedom, who had used the stadium for mass baptisms and sermons, played *Auld Lang Syne* to say goodbye to the old ballpark.

"A stadium was laid to rest yesterday," *Washington Post* sports editor Shirley Povich wrote in the next day's paper. "Not many showed up for the services and the deceased was not much of a draw."

Despite their second-half collapse, the Senators actually had a chance to finish out of the cellar, which would have been a decent accomplishment for an expansion team. Going into the season finale in Kansas City with the last-place Athletics, Washington held a one-game lead over the A's. But Kansas City won the game, 3–2, and the two teams finished in a last-place tie—with 61–100 records (.379), 47½ games out of first. After its impressive 30–30 start,

Washington went 30–71 over its last 101 games, less than a .300 clip. The team finished eight games behind the other expansion team, the Los Angeles Angels.

The season was a failure by another barometer. The Twins finished 8½ games ahead of the new Senators, and more importantly, drew 1.26 million fans—double Washington's 597,000, and more than they had ever drawn in Washington.

After the season, the Senators acquired Jimmy Piersall from the Cleveland Indians for Washington's starting catcher, Gene Green, who had led the team in home runs with 18; pitcher Dick Donovan, who had a league-best 2.40 ERA; and utility infielder Jim Mahoney. Piersall's book about his mental illness, *Fear Strikes Out*, had been turned into a movie in 1957 and had caused quite a stir in baseball.

Piersall was one of the best defensive outfielders in the game, and was coming off a career-year offensively in which he hit .322. During a visit to Washington in the off-season, the colorful Piersall said he wasn't disappointed about getting traded to a last-place team. "If you're not traded to the Yankees, what's the difference?" he said. "Anyway, I was glad to get away from Cleveland and those Cleveland writers."

On April 9, 1962, Washington played its first game at its new state-of-the-art D.C. Stadium, with ticket prices the same as the old Griffith Stadium: $3 for box seats, $2.50 for reserved grandstand seats, and $1.50 for unreserved grandstand seats. The ballpark, paid for with federal funds, had a futuristic feel to it, with a sloped top that made it look like a UFO.

The Senators got the place off to a good start, winning 4–1. President Kennedy, who again threw out the first ball, told team president Quesada and General Manager Doherty, "I'm leaving you in first place."

But the Senators didn't stay there for long. In fact, eight games into the 1962 season, they were in last place, a position they would hold for most of the year. This time, Washington would have the bottom all to itself—finishing 60–101, 35½ games out of first—a game off its 1961 pace. The team even finished 11½ games behind the next-worst team, the Athletics. Meanwhile, the Angels were showing that an expansion team could have some success, finishing with a winning record, in third place.

The Twins rubbed it in some more, catapulting to second place, just five games behind the first-place Yankees, leading Washington fans to wonder what would have been if the old Senators had just stayed put for a couple of more seasons. The new Senators did improve in one important category—drawing 729,000 fans, an increase of nearly 150,000 from 1961, as they enjoyed the benefits of playing in a new ballpark.

Another highlight for Washington: playing host to the 1962 All-Star Game. Its fans got to see such legends as Willie Mays, Orlando Cepeda, Roberto Clemente, Mickey Mantle, Roger Maris, Stan Musial, Juan Marichal, and Jim Bunning in one game. The sole Senators representative, pitcher Dave Stenhouse, did not play, reinforcing the team's sense of futility.

But a Washington native literally stole the show that day. Los Angeles Dodgers speedster Maury Wills, who grew up in the projects of Northeast Washington, entered the game as a pinch-runner for Musial in the sixth inning of a scoreless game. Wills quickly stole second base, then scored the game's first run on a Dick Groat single.

With the National League up 2–1 in the eighth inning, Wills used his aggressiveness to manufacture an insurance run. After leading off the frame with a single, Wills took a wide turn around second base on a single by Jim Davenport. Left fielder Rocky Colavito threw to second base, but Wills took off for third, and slid under the tag of the relay throw from second. He then scored on a sacrifice fly.

For his exploits, Wills won the game's Most Valuable Player Award, but the day didn't start out that great for him. Because he still had relatives in the city, he stayed with them rather than at the team hotel, and when he arrived at the ballpark, the team was already there.

"When I got there with my Dodger duffle bag, the clubhouse attendant wouldn't let me in," Wills recalls. "He didn't believe I was a baseball player. I showed him my Dodger bag—he still wouldn't let me in—I was too little." Wills is about five feet 10 inches tall.

"I said, 'I am a Dodger player, and I'll prove it to you. Open the door, and the guys inside will tell you.' So he opened the door, and yelled, 'Anybody inside know this guy?' And baseball players have a sick sense of humor, and they all looked at me and said, 'Never saw him before.' And he said, 'I knew it, get out of here!'" Eventually, Wills made his way in to the clubhouse.

"After the game, I walked out with the MVP trophy and showed it to him, and he still doesn't believe I'm a baseball player," Wills recalls with a laugh.

Wills had his greatest year in 1962. He set a single-season record with 104 stolen bases, since broken, and hit .299 with 10 triples.

From 1959 to 1962, baseball staged two All-Star games a year, and in the second one that season, Washington's Stenhouse not only played, but started for the American League. Unfortunately, the game was at Chicago's Wrigley

Field, so few Washington fans could see the action in person. Stenhouse pitched two innings, giving up one run on three hits and one walk. He finished the season as the team leader in wins, going 11–12 with a 3.65 ERA.

By September, the Senators were already 30 games under .500, but still managed to put together some memorable moments. On September 5, the aptly named Washington Senator John Kennedy slammed a home run in his first major league at bat—and broke up a no-hitter by Minnesota's Dick Stigman in the process.

"He circled the bases like he was running a hundred-yard dash," Manager Mickey Vernon recalls. "He was white as a ghost."

Kennedy says he ran so hard he could hardly breathe by the time he got back to the dugout. "I went around the bases in a sprint," he says. "I was really excited. That was the biggest home run. I always felt that when you hit a ball, you ran. Nowadays, guys watch the ball, hoping it will sail out of ballpark. I was taught to run as hard as I can."

One week later, Senators pitcher Tom Cheney set a major league record for most strikeouts in a major league game, fanning 21 batters in a 16-inning, 2–1 victory over the Baltimore Orioles. Cheney made over 200 pitches, twice the count that would get him yanked nowadays. Baltimore third baseman Brooks Robinson said after the game: "You know, there were times I never saw the ball."

There was more excitement in Baltimore the next night, when Senators outfielder Jimmy Piersall jumped into the stands to confront a fan who had taunted him about his history of mental illness. "This guy was on my back while we were in batting practice," Piersall said after the game. "He was calling me things like 'crazy man,' and said I should be in Spring Grove. I didn't know what he was talking about but later I learned that Spring Grove is a Baltimore mental institution.

"I told him to come down to the field and say those things. He told me: 'You come up here.' So I did. But I never touched him." Both Piersall and the fan were hauled off to the Baltimore police station. Piersall was charged with disorderly conduct but was not convicted.

Shaking things up in the final days of the season, Quesada fired general manager Doherty and rehired manager Vernon—the opposite of what was expected. Two months later, Quesada hired George Selkirk as general manager. Selkirk had played for the Yankees back in the 1930s and '40s, taking Babe Ruth's place in the outfield. The new GM came in with an aggressive attitude.

"I will trade with anybody," he said. "I don't believe in untouchables. The only 'Untouchables' are in television. We'll make any deal that will help the club."

There were more big changes for the franchise in the off-season. In January, 1963, Quesada sold his one-tenth interest in the team and relinquished his presidency, but not before writing a three-part report to the "Greater Washington Baseball Public" slamming sportswriters Povich of the *Post* and Morris Siegel of the *Washington Star* for alleged distortions.

Povich, getting the last word in, wrote, "It was France's Clemenceau who once observed, 'War is too important to be entrusted to generals.' So, perhaps, is baseball."

Bill Gilbert, who was fired by Quesada after serving as the team's marketing director for two years, described him as a micromanaging executive who once invited local disc jockeys to lunch, only to ask them to omit rainy forecasts when the team was home. He also argued that Quesada set the stage for the team's move a decade later by signing only a 10-year lease with RFK, as opposed to the Redskins, who inked a 30-year deal.

A group headed by former Cleveland Indians co-owners Nate Dolin and Bill Veeck made a $5 million offer for the team—a healthy markup from the $3 million price two years earlier. But instead five of the original 10 stockholders bought out the other five, and investment banker James M. Johnston took over as the new board chairman.

In May 1963, Selkirk fired Vernon, the team's manager since its inception, and replaced him with Gil Hodges, a former star first baseman for the Brooklyn and Los Angeles Dodgers. To get Hodges, who was finishing his playing career with the Mets, the Senators traded Piersall to New York. In his two seasons in Washington, Piersall had hit just .244 and .245.

Selkirk said he was sorry to fire the popular Vernon. "The last thing I wanted to do is what I'm doing," he said. "But I don't want to finish last. This club isn't hustling. The players haven't hustled all year."

Taking over a team with a 14–27 record, Hodges couldn't turn things around. He lost his first four games as manager, and eight of his first nine games. The team solidified its hold on last place, finishing 56–106 (.346), the worst record of the new Senators, and 14½ games out of ninth place—not to mention 48½ games out of first place. Only 536,000 fans came out that season, also a low for the expansion Senators.

Washington hit an anemic .227 that year, with no regular batting over .270. Outfielder Chuck Hinton, who had hit .310 in 1962, slumped to .269, still a team-best. Don Lock, another outfielder, led the team with 27 homers, but hit only .252. The team's pitching wasn't much better, compiling a 4.42 ERA, but two starters had stellar years. Tom Cheney had a team-best 2.71 ERA, although poor run support got him just an 8–9 record. Southpaw Claude Osteen won a team-high nine games, losing 14 despite a 3.35 ERA.

Manager Mickey Vernon (right) greets Cuban great Minnie Minoso in 1963. Rucker Archive

After three straight last-place finishes, the franchise decided not to aim too high for the following season. The cover of its 1964 yearbook had this inspiring rallying cry: "Off The Floor—in '64!" A cartoon showed an over-sized, muscle-bound player with "American League" written across his chest, being tugged at by a child-sized player in a Senators uniform, who says, "I'm out to get you this year, fella!"

Washington barely met its modest goal, finishing in ninth place, with its best record—62–100 (.383), four percentage points ahead of its previous best, in 1961. Claude Osteen, turning into a bona fide ace, won 15 games with a 3.33 ERA.

But the hitting continued to be awful. The Senators batted just .231 as a team, and no regular hit over .275. Washington's offense took several days off in early September, failing to score in four consecutive games.

"The first man who scores a run for the Senators," wrote *Washington Post* sportswriter Bob Addie, "should rank among the great trailblazers of history, such as Pere Marquette, Columbus, the Wright Brothers and the Beatles." The streak matched one by the old Senators, who had lost four straight games by identical scores of 2–0 in 1958.

Still, getting out of last place was an accomplishment. Pitcher Jim Hannan recalls the team celebrating after clinching a ninth-place finish: "We had a little champagne and a party like you won the World Series. It was sort of tongue-in-cheek, I think, but we enjoyed it."

The *Star* asked, "And next year's motto? How about 'Still Alive in Sixty-Five?'"

The Senators made several moves after the '64 season to improve the club. In a blockbuster deal, they traded Claude Osteen and John Kennedy to the Dodgers for slugger Frank Howard and four other players. Howard, a six-foot-seven-inch behemoth, blossomed in Washington and became a fan favorite. He left behind a team that had won the 1963 World Series and would win the championship again in 1965. In the fourth and final game of the '63 series, Howard's single and homer were the only hits the Dodgers managed off Yankees pitcher Whitey Ford, but they were enough to propel Los Angeles to a 2–1 win and complete the series sweep.

Howard says it was a worthy trade-off to get to play every day. In Los Angeles, he usually got between 400 and 500 at bats a season, and he was coming off his worst year in '64, batting just .226 with 24 home runs. After the trade, "I got a chance to get another 150 at bats, and I had my best years here," says Howard, who still lives in the Washington area.

Howard provided some thump to what had been a listless offense. In his first year in Washington, he led the team in batting (.289), home runs (21), and RBIs (84)—the kind of production the Senators sorely needed. "We have to go for numbers," GM Selkirk said after announcing the deal. "Everybody knows about Howard. He's still young enough (28) and Gil Hodges and I think he's one of the most powerful hitters in the game."

Meanwhile, the ownership continued to consolidate. The partners in the investment firm of Johnston, Lemon & Co.—board chairman James M. Johnston and James H. Lemon—bought out the stock of the remaining team owners to take full control of the team in January 1965. Johnston said that he had received many offers to sell, but wanted to retain ownership to ensure the team would stay in Washington.

For the second straight season, Washington climbed gradually in the standings. The team finished in eighth place, with a 70–92 record—both bests for the new franchise. The trade with the Dodgers paid off for Washington, and not just because of Frank Howard. Southpaw pitcher Pete Richert, also acquired in the deal, stepped into the role of new staff ace, compiling a 15–12 record and a 2.60 ERA. Another acquisition, third baseman Ken McMullen, hit .263 with 18 homers, second to Howard in both categories.

One low point, at least emotionally, came on the last weekend of September. The city's old team, the Twins, came back home to clinch their first American League pennant, defeating the Senators, 2–1, at D.C. Stadium on September 26. It was the franchise's first pennant since 1933.

"Calvin Griffith's band of displaced athletes left here paupers in 1961. They returned as princes of the baseball realm," wrote Addie. The win climaxed a three-game sweep, giving Minnesota a 15–3 margin in head-to-head games that year—more than enough to help the Twins win the pennant by seven games.

"Few teams did more to give the old Senators, or Twins, an assist toward the championship than did the present denizens of D.C. Stadium," the *Star* wrote in an editorial. The Twins celebrated on the Senators' turf, swimming in champagne, and taking a congratulatory call from Vice President Hubert Humphrey—a transplanted Minnesotan in the nation's capital.

Still, there was reason for optimism in Washington. The team had improved for two straight seasons under manager Gil Hodges, who predicted the team could finish in the "first division"—or top half of the standings—in 1966. "This will be our goal," he wrote in the *Star*. "I believe we can do it if some of our younger fellows come along as well as we expect them to."

Hodges said he wanted bigger things from his big man. Frank Howard had put up decent numbers in 1965, Hodges wrote, "but Frank is 6-foot-7 and weighs 255 pounds, so fans expect more of him. He's capable of doing much more."

But Howard wound up with his lowest home run and RBI totals in a Washington uniform in 1966, hitting just 18 round-trippers and knocking in a mere 71.

Howard did hit one of the most memorable home runs in Washington baseball history that year. In a 3–2 loss to the White Sox in April, he slammed a ball into the upper deck in center field at D.C. Stadium, a colossal shot some players said would have traveled farther than any ball in history had it not been hit in an enclosed ballpark.

"Frank Howard hit that ball like a two-iron right back at the pitcher, who actually fell down on the ground," recalls Senators outfielder Fred Valentine. "And Tommie Agee was playing center field, and he started in, but the ball just kept rising and it wound up in the upper deck. Nobody could believe it."

On July 8, the Senators went to New York to play a five-game weekend series against the Yankees, starting with a doubleheader Friday night. Washington pitcher Jim Hannan was scheduled to pitch the opening game, but Hannan, a New Jersey native, persuaded Hodges to let him pitch the second game so his family could come out and watch him pitch in prime time at Yankee Stadium.

In the third inning, Hannan gave up a home run to Mickey Mantle that rivaled Howard's two months earlier. "Mantle at one point was 19-for-21 off me," Hannan says. "So I say, 'Well, if he hits it, he's gonna have to hit it out in centerfield. 'Cause I'm pitching it out over the plate.' So I throw it out over the plate. He hits it. Centerfielder turns around. And I said, 'Oh my God, over the monuments. Oh my God, over the backdrop. Oh my God, it's gonna go out of the stadium.'" The ball did stay in the ballpark, landing in the bleachers an estimated 461 feet away.

Hannan recalls a testy exchange with Hodges on the mound after that: "He comes out and he says nothing. He put his hand out, and he had huge hands. And I'm thinking, 'Son of a bitch, if he's not gonna ask me for the ball, I'm not giving it to him.' Gil never wanted to show anyone up and never wanted to be showed up. Well, I'm turned around and I'm showing him up. I don't hand him the ball. I turn around and I just hold the ball.

"And he grabs me by the elbow with the other hand and just starts crunching it. And he says, 'If you don't give me that damn ball, it's gonna be $500 and . . . and . . . ' And, I said to myself, 'OK, he talked to me.' I turned around and gave him the ball." Washington wound up losing the game, 7–5, blowing a 4–0 lead. But the Senators took four out of five games in the series.

Despite Hodge's preseason optimism, Washington only marginally improved in 1966. The team finished in eighth place again, with a 71–88 record (.447). The Senators' hitting woes continued, as they hit just .234 as a team. Howard's modest .278 average was the best of any regular.

After the season, Washington shipped standout reliever Ron Kline to the Minnesota Twins for an old Senators pitching star, Camilo Pascual, and infielder Bernie Allen. Kline had led the Senators with 23 saves and a 2.39 ERA. Pascual, a Cuban find by Senators scout Joe Cambria, had won 20 games twice with the Twins, but he was coming off a bad season (8–6, 4.89 ERA). He bounced back for the Senators in 1967, winning a team-high 12 games while posting a 3.28 ERA.

Hodges entered the 1967 season determined to improve the Senators' woeful offense. "Our pitching will be as strong, if not stronger than last year," he said at the beginning of spring training. "And last year our pitching did a fine job." But he noted the team finished last in runs scored in '66.

"I looked it up because I couldn't quite believe it," he said. "We have to master a better attack, that's all there is to it." Despite Hodges' best efforts, Washington's offense would not improve in 1967. But the Senators would give their fans an exciting season.

In an effort to upgrade their offense, two months into the season the Senators traded their ace pitcher, Pete Richert, to the Baltimore Orioles for the highly touted slugging prospect Mike Epstein and pitcher Frank Bertaina. Epstein, 24, had been named *Sporting News* Minor League Player of the Year the previous season after hitting .309 with 29 homers and 102 RBIs at Rochester. But when Baltimore tried to send him down again at the end of spring training in 1967, he balked, saying he was returning to college. The Orioles, the defending World Series champions, already had Boog Powell at first base, and weren't able to convert Epstein from a first baseman to an outfielder.

A week after the trade, the six-foot-three-inch, 230-pound Epstein made his Senators debut in an unexpected way—by hitting an inside-the-park home run at Yankee Stadium. The 200-foot blast came after Epstein visited his grandmother just a few blocks from the ballpark.

In June, the Senators began an unbelievable stretch of extra-inning games, starting with a 7–5, 19-inning loss to the Orioles on June 4. Washington scored five runs in the top of the third inning, then put up goose eggs for the next 16. Baltimore won the game on a two-run homer by Andy Etchebarren in the bottom of the 19th. The loss spoiled a great pitching performance by the Senators' bullpen, which during one 11-inning stretch surrendered just one infield hit.

In that game, Hodges tried out a new shift against Orioles slugger and future Nationals manager Frank Robinson. Hodges used his second baseman as a fourth outfielder in the 15th and 18th innings, and Robinson went 0-for-2 against the softball-style defense.

Just eight days later, the Senators proved they were mastering the art of the filibuster set by their namesakes a mile away on Capitol Hill. They lasted for 22 innings against the Chicago White Sox, finally winning, 6–5, on a bases-loaded single by catcher Paul Casanova—his first hit in nine at bats. More impressive, Casanova caught all 22 innings, after catching the full 19-innings game the week before.

"I could have played 30 innings," he said after the six-hour, thirty-eight-minute game. "I wasn't tired. I could have gone all night."

Or all morning. Sunrise was just a few hours away when Casanova knocked in the winning run at 2:44 a.m. with 2,000 fans still on hand. "The fans were forever yelling and clapping," recalls Fred Valentine, who played the whole game in center field and went 2-for-9. "At that time, you could bring your coolers in, and most of them were boozed up. But they stayed, and that shows how much they supported the team."

The Senators excited their fans with more than extra-inning games that season. In July, they climbed from tenth place to seventh after winning eight straight games. "The last time they could boast of anything near their current achievement was in 1949, when Harry Truman was living at 1600 Pennsylvania Avenue," wrote *Star* sportswriter Morris Siegel. "All of a sudden Washington has become interested in something besides how many chowhounds the Redskins are assembling at Carlisle, Pa., for the imminent opening of Camp Runamuck."

Washington was still five games under .500 at the end of the streak, but they finally reached the break-even point with a 5–0 victory over the Twins on August 7. After dropping the second game of the series, the Senators climbed back to .500 the next night—and morning. For the third time of the year, Washington played a single game that went more than double the length of a normal game, beating the Twins, 9–7, in 20 innings.

Trailing 7–0 with two outs in the seventh inning, Washington rallied for seven runs to tie the game. The Senators' bats cooled off as quickly as they had heated up, going scoreless for the next 11 innings before winning the game on a home run by Ken McMullen in the top of the 20th.

Washington, which had been 14½ games out of first place a month earlier, had now climbed within 6½ games from the top. Fans started calling the team to ask about World Series tickets. When the Senators came home a week later, they were still at .500, but that was more than enough for their long-suffering fans. Four thousand Senators rooters were waiting at National Airport to welcome the team back from a successful road trip. Now Washington was just six games out of first place. Both fans and players were talking about making a run for the pennant.

More than 27,000 fans came out to see the Senators open a home stand and crucial three-game series against the Cleveland Indians. For six innings, a pitching duel between Washington's Barry Moore and Cleveland's Stan Williams kept both teams scoreless. But the Indians rallied for three runs in the top of the seventh inning, and held on for a 3–0 victory. Washington bats remained dormant the next night, and the team fell, 1–0.

In the third and final game of the series, Frank Howard ended the team's scoreless streak at 28 innings with a home run in the third. The Senators added two more runs in the frame to build a 3–0 lead. But Cleveland eventually tied the game, and once again Washington was to play its signature '67 game—an extra-inning contest. Unfortunately, the offense returned to its comatose condition, failing to score over the game's final 13 innings. Cleveland finally won the game with five runs in the top of the 16th. In the demoralizing series, Washington scored just three runs in 34 innings, and was on its way to a 2–9 tailspin. By the end of August, the team's pennant run was effectively over.

Washington finished 76–85, good for a franchise-best .472 winning percentage. The team also had its highest finish in the standings, a tie for sixth place with the Orioles, the previous year's world champs. And Washington drew a franchise record 771,000.

The team was improving overall, but its offense was not. Washington hit just .223 as a team, last in the American League. Its double-play combination was particularly impotent. Second baseman Bernie Allen hit .193 with three homers and 18 RBIs in 87 games, while shortstop Ed Brinkman batted just .188 with one homer and 18 RBIs in 109 games. Slugging first baseman Mike Epstein failed to provide the pop Washington had hoped for, finishing with a .229 average, nine homers, and 29 RBIs. But Frank Howard was finally emerging as the player many thought he could be. Following Hodges's advice, the big slugger opened his stance, and set a new career-high with 36 home runs.

The disappointing finish continued into the off-season, when manager Gil Hodges quit to take the manager's job with the New York Mets. Because Hodges had one year left on his contract, the Mets agreed to pay cash and send pitcher Bill Denehy to the Senators as compensation, but Denehy would pitch just two innings for Washington. Hodges had nudged the Senators up the standings every season after his first year, but the lure of playing for his hometown team and a generous salary proved too much to resist.

"The Mets were desperate, and, besides, they can afford it," wrote Shirley Povich. "The Senators liked their manager and believed that now he had the Washington team rolling with his sixth-place finish. But the Senators found themselves helpless against baseball's code of the jungle, the honorless system that condones this form of wife-stealing by the Mets or any other team."

Senators pitcher Jim Hannan recalls hearing the news in New York, where he worked as a stockbroker on Wall Street in the off-season. He told his Met fan co-workers: "'Boy you guys have got the greatest coaching staff in the world. You guys, the Mets, will win the World Series in a year or two.' And they thought I was crazy. They said, 'What? The Mets?' I said, 'You wait and see. You got young pitchers by the name of Tom Seaver, Jerry Koosman, Nolan Ryan. They're going to be great pitchers someday. And you're getting a coaching staff that knows how to handle them.'"

Hodges was taking over a team that had finished in tenth place the previous season. It took him a little time to turn things around—in 1968 New York finished ninth—but the Miracle Mets won the World Series the next year.

Meanwhile, Washington turned to Jim Lemon (no relation to the owner) as its new manager. Lemon had played for the old Senators team for six seasons, hitting 38 home runs in the team's final year in Washington, before moving with the franchise to Minnesota. He had spent the last three seasons as the Twins' first base coach.

In December, the board chairman, James M. Johnston, died of cancer at the age of 72, leaving his investment bank partner, James M. Lemon, in control of the team. Johnston had expressed a philosophical attitude about the lack of profitability in owning the Senators, once remarking, "It's too bad it costs me money but I suppose you have to pay the piper. I must love the game to put so much money into it—especially since I'm a Scotsman."

Within a year, the team would be put up for sale. And unfortunately for the Senators, their next owner would not have the same attitude as the old Scotsman.

In 1968, riots enveloped the nation's capital following the assassination of Martin Luther King, Jr., forcing the postponement of the home opener by two days. Across the city, businesses closed out of mourning for the civil rights leader, and officials imposed curfews to stem the rioting. One of the National Guard soldiers helping to restore order was Senators' shortstop Ed Brinkman, who missed nearly half the 1967 and 1968 seasons for guard duty.

"I'd be with the club, traveling, and the phone would ring, and they'd say, 'There's going to be 30-thousand kids rioting against the Vietnam War this weekend, and you've got to come back,'" he recalls.

In 1968, Brinkman says, he patrolled the city to keep people off the streets during curfew. "I was stationed in a firehouse for a while, because the firemen were going out to all of these fires that people were setting across the city, and the people were ruining the equipment," he says. "So they took some of the National Guard guys and put us each in a firehouse so we could protect the hoses and the gear. I hadn't realized when I signed up that Washington, D.C., is probably the worst place to join the National Guard—there's always something going on."

When the Senators finally opened their season on April 10, 1968, Brinkman was at the game—but in the stands in his Army uniform, yelling taunts down at his buddy and roommate, Frank Howard, in left field.

"The game's going on, and I'm trying to concentrate, and he's hollering at me," Howard recalls with a laugh. "I'm thinking, if we have to depend upon this guy to save us, we're in deep trouble."

The tense situation in the city kept the attendance to just 32,000 people, well short of a sellout. Vice President Hubert Humphrey, filling in for President Lyndon B. Johnson, threw out the first ball, but the Minnesotan was booed when he walked over to the Twins dugout to greet his favorite team. The Twins won, 2–0, wasting a good effort by Senators pitcher Camilo Pascual.

Things didn't get much better for Washington that season. The team slumped to a last-place finish—reversing several years of progress made under Hodges—and drew just 542,000 fans.

Jim Hannan was one of only two pitchers on the staff with a winning record, going 10–6 with a 3.01 ERA (the other was Pascual, who went 13–12 with a 2.69 ERA). But Hannan's most memorable record that year was not his winning percentage, but his strikeout streak—as a hitter. He fanned 13 straight times, but says there's more to the story.

"The coaches thought I was getting tired running the bases, so they didn't want me to get on base," he recalls. "Now four or five of those strikeouts I got on my own, but I went two or three games where I wasn't allowed to swing at a ball. So I was always trying to get a walk—I'd get a 3-and-2 count, and I'd start thinking, 'What's going to happen if I get a walk?'"

Finally, Hannan says, he went to the coaching staff and said, "This is getting embarrassing. It's one thing not getting on base, but just striking out? I'm setting records here. Can I please just swing and hit the ball? I promise you I will not get on base.'" The edict was lifted. Hannan finished the year with just three hits and an .064 batting average.

Frank Howard offered fans something to cheer for that season. In May, the "Capital Punisher" tied an American League record with home runs in six straight games—walloping an astonishing 10 dingers over the period in 20 at bats.

He capped it with a 550-foot-blast in Detroit, which landed on top of the grandstand and bounced out of the stadium, one of two home runs he hit that day off Tigers hurler Mickey Lolich, the same pitcher Howard had begun his streak off a week earlier. Howard became only the second player to clear the left-field stands at Tiger Stadium; the first was former Senator Harmon Killebrew, who accomplished the feat as a Minnesota Twin in 1962. Cecil Fielder became the third and final player to do it in 1993 before the Tigers moved to Comerica Park.

"You know when you put a good swing on the baseball—there's no pressure, no white-knuckle effect where there's tension in your swing," Howard recalls. "It's just a free swing, a smooth swing, a quick swing. I didn't know it went over the roof until I got back to the dugout. You couldn't stand and admire the ball in those days. You're asking to get clipped if you did. That's one thing you couldn't do—you couldn't show the pitcher up out there. He'll put a little part in your hair next time. It's like digging a hole in that batter's box—and Bob Gibson or Don Drysdale would bury you in it."

Howard remembers being ice cold in the two series before the streak, when the Yankees and Red Sox came to Washington. "It's like a water tap," he says. "You can't turn that hot water on and turn it off—you've got to try to keep that water running all the time."

Howard, who had benefited from opening his stance a year earlier under Hodges, further refined his stance under Lemon, by moving in closer to the plate. He led the league that season with a career-high 44 home runs.

But overall, the team's hitting did not improve. True, this was the "Year of the Pitcher," when offense was down so much that the National League won the All-Star Game, 1–0, and Carl Yastrzemski won the American League batting crown with just a .301 average. Even by '68 standards, however, the Senators were seriously subpar. They hit just .224 as a team, second-to-last in the league (to the Yankees, who hit .214). Howard, who hit .274, was the only Washington regular to bat over .250. The pitching wasn't much better, as the Senators' pitching staff finished with a league-worst 3.64 ERA.

The 1968 season marked the end of an era for the Washington Senators. By the next year, the team would have a new owner and new manager, and some enthusiasm for a rejuvenated franchise. But the change in ownership ultimately led to Washington losing yet another baseball team.

EIGHT

A SHORT RUN:
THE TED WILLIAMS ERA

A SHORT RUN: THE TED WILLIAMS ERA

Big changes were in store for the Senators after the disappointing 1968 season. Owner James H. Lemon put the team up for sale, and two men emerged as the leading bidders: comedian Bob Hope and wealthy Minnesota businessman Robert E. Short. Hope talked about including other stars as partners, such as Johnny Carson and Steve McQueen. "Maybe we will conduct the whole baseball operation through the Screen Actors Guild," he joked.

But in the end, Minnesotan money won out over Hollywood glitter, as Short, a hotel and trucking executive, bought the team for $9.4 million. Short was already deeply immersed in Washington politics, having served as treasurer of the Democratic National Committee and chief fundraiser for Hubert Humphrey's failed 1968 presidential campaign. Back then, there were no campaign finance laws limiting political donations, and Short gave the campaign $125,000. He also ran unsuccessfully for the U.S. House and Minnesota lieutenant governor.

In an editorial, the *Washington Post* suggested that Short and Hope may have been baseball proxies for the presidential candidates that year—Democrat Humphrey and Republican Richard Nixon: "Robert Short is a Democrat and a friend of Hubert Humphrey—to whose campaign he was a financial contributor. Bob Hope, on the other hand, is a Republican and a friend of Richard Nixon—to whose campaign he was a financial contributor. We all know how that particular contest came out; but lately the two men have been waging a second campaign against each other, not for the presidency this time, but for ownership of the Washington Senators—a sort of baseball team."

Short was no stranger to sports, either. He bought the Minneapolis Lakers in 1957, but moved them to Los Angeles in 1960, right around the time the first Senators had left Washington for Minnesota—an ominous sign for a city trying to hold on to baseball. Short, who had bought the Lakers for $300,000, sold them in 1965 to Jack Kent Cooke for more than $5 million. Cooke, ironically, would later become owner of the Washington Redskins. At the time of the Senators purchase, Short owned a 1 percent share in the Twins, but sold it as required by baseball rules.

Also ominous was a comment Short made to the *Post* after purchasing the Senators, about his negotiations with Webb C. Hayes III, the team's executive vice president and counsel: "I refused to sign any papers that would prevent me from moving the club out of Washington. I told Hayes that I wasn't buying the team to move it. But, legally, I wanted the right to move it if it ever became necessary."

Famed slugger Ted Williams as the Senators' manager. Rucker Archive.

Short had an ambitious master plan for the franchise: out of last place in 1969, in the top half of the standings in 1970, a pennant contender team in 1971, and in the World Series no later than 1972. He would meet only the first goal.

At a press conference at D.C. Stadium, Short said he wanted to see improvements made to the ballpark. "From the outside, it's beautiful. But from the inside, it's dirty. The house-keeping is not as it should be. We should pay enough rent so the place could be clean inside. At least, the concrete could be painted and whitewashed."

He said that his long-range plans for the stadium included "VIP Club seats," which would become standard in baseball years after the Senators had moved away. On a more pressing matter, Short said, "I don't want them running out of hot dogs when they know they're going to have a full stadium." (That's exactly what happened 38 years later, when a full house came out to see the first Nationals home game in 2005.) Finally, Short promised: "We're not going to have any cellar club next year." The team was coming off a last-place finish, 31 games under .500.

As one of his first moves, Short vetoed a trade that would have sent catcher Paul Casanova and first baseman Mike Epstein to Atlanta for catcher Joe Torre. That turned out to be a blunder. The Braves instead shipped Torre to the St. Louis Cardinals, where he knocked in more than 100 runs in each of the next three seasons, including a monster 1971 season when he won the Most Valuable Player award with a .363 average and 137 RBIs. Epstein did have a career year in 1969, slamming 30 homers and knocking in 85 runs, but he trailed off the following season before being traded in 1971. Casanova would never hit higher than .230 for the rest of his career.

Then Short fired George Selkirk, the team's general manager since 1962, and team manager Jim Lemon, who had been skipper for only one year. And the new owner raised ticket prices—the best seats in the house were jacked up from $4 to $5; the cheapest from $1.50 to $2.

But the biggest move was yet to come.

In February 1969, Short announced his new manager—Hall-of-Famer Ted Williams, who had been out of baseball since retiring after the 1960 season. The "Splendid Splinter" inked himself a splendid contract—five years at $65,000 a year, plus a deferred option to buy 10 percent of the team. It was the best deal for a manager at the time. A reporter asked Williams if he would "tolerate a player with a temperament like Ted Williams had as a player." Responded Ted: "If he can hit like Ted Williams, yes."

Williams's initial answer to the job offer was "Nooooo," Short recalled in a 1970 *Washingtonian* profile on the new manager.

"So then I told him I thought he had a responsibility toward the game, toward the country, toward Nixon, and the whole bunch of bull you throw into a business proposition," Short said. "He said: 'I'll tell you what I'll do. Goddamn it, I know you're in a hell of a fix. I can't do it, but I'll help you find somebody.' I knew I had him in the bag then. As long as he's going to draw up lists of who might do the job, it's going to come out just like my list. Ted Williams has to come out on top. And that's what happened."

Short's specific appeal to Nixon was no coincidence. Williams was a big admirer of the new president, and would even post a grainy photo of Nixon in his office as manager.

Williams's reputation included an adversarial relationship with the press, dating back to his time as an outfielder with the Red Sox. "But by the time he was manager, he was great, he was spellbinding," says former *Washington Post* sports editor George Solomon, who was a columnist for the now-defunct *Washington Daily News* at the time. "You'd sit in lobbies with him, and he would spin tales and talk about Joe DiMaggio and Bob Feller and the great pitchers and great hitters. He was just so interesting. If you were interested enough to ask, he'd be interested enough to talk about it forever."

Short's son, Brian, says that his late father wanted someone with star power to lead the team. "Ted Williams was a star, and my father thought people would buy tickets to the games because of him," Brian Short says. "My father was a promotional genius. Major league owners were a stodgy group. Their view was you didn't have to promote, because it was the national pastime."

That season, the American League split into two divisions to accommodate its first expansion since the Senators had entered the league. Unfortunately for Washington, the two expansion teams, the Seattle Pilots and the Kansas City Royals, were put in the Western Division, so the Senators would not have a couple of easy teams to beat out in their Eastern Division. Washington was grouped with the Red Sox, Indians, Tigers, Yankees, and Orioles.

Bill Gildea, who covered the Senators for the *Post* at the time, went down to the Florida Keys to interview Williams at his home there, and was struck by how removed the new manager was from the game. "He didn't know who was on the team," Gildea recalls. "He didn't know the league was split into divisions. He was trying to get in his head around how the White Sox could be in the Western Division."

Inheriting a team that had hit just .224 the previous year, the new manager went to work to try to build up the offense. One player who needed a lot of improvement was shortstop Eddie Brinkman, whose consistency over the past two seasons would have been impressive—if it hadn't been so consistently bad. Brinkman had hit .188 in 1967 and .187 in 1968. When Brinkman arrived at spring training at Pompano Beach, Williams greeted the six-foot, 150-pound short-stop by saying, "Hey, you're even skinnier than I thought you were!"

"I just walked away, thinking, 'Oh my,'" Brinkman recalls.

Later, Williams told Brinkman not to take a glove with him on the field. "If I ever see you with a glove on your hand in the first two or three weeks of spring training, I'm going to hit you over the head with a damn bat," Williams said. "They tell me you can catch the ball, but your weakness is hitting. So carry your bat with you every place you go."

So for two weeks, Brinkman left his glove behind and focused exclusively on hitting. Finally, the day before the first spring training game, Brinkman asked his manager if he would be in the lineup.

"Yeah!" Williams barked.

"You know," Brinkman replied, "I haven't fielded a ground ball yet. I haven't taken my glove out of my locker."

"Oh, geez, you better get it, then, and field some ground balls."

Brinkman says that Williams was adept at getting players to increase their focus at the plate:

> "What he helped me with most was the mental part, not so much the physical stuff: 'Get a good pitch to hit. Don't swing at the bad balls.' He was always by the batting cage, and if you didn't concentrate at all times—if you hit the ball up against the cage or beat one down in the dirt—he'd jump all over you: 'Hey!' he'd scream. And his voice carried even when he wasn't screaming. 'Wait on the ball! Get on top of the ball! What the hell were you thinking up there?!' It really bothered him when you swung at bad pitches.
>
> "So just by him doing that, you would concentrate like crazy, just during batting practice. For me, it would carry over into the game, and I hit a little bit better. I was never going to win a batting title, but I became a better hitter. The concentration level really went up a lot."

But Brinkman had another problem: he had missed about half the games the previous two seasons because of National Guard duty, making it difficult for him to find a rhythm. When he told Williams that he had to report for duty when the team returned north, the manager was furious. Military service during World War II and the Korean War service had cut into Williams's own playing career.

Brinkman recalls Williams's reaction: "They ain't going to mess around with my players. They messed around with me for six years; they ain't going to mess around with my players, blah, blah, blah."

So Williams arranged for Brinkman and team representatives to meet with military officials at the D.C. Armory, located across the street from the stadium. They worked out a deal where Brinkman would work at the Armory when the team was home, from 6 a.m. to 4 p.m., then go the ballpark to play at night.

"The team trainer had an old rollaway bed in the clubhouse," Brinkman recalls. "So I'd get over there at 4 or 4:30 in the afternoon, and go in the back. I'd lay down on that rollaway bed and sleep for a couple of hours. This was pretty much every day when we were home, with the exception of weekends. So I never missed any games in 1969. When I went on the road, I didn't have to come back for guard duty."

The increased focus that came from Williams's coaching, as well as playing every day, paid off. In 1969, Brinkman raised his batting average by 79 points to .266.

Williams didn't limit his coaching to the weak hitters. He also jumped on the team's best hitter, Frank Howard, summoning the slugger to the manager's office on the third day of spring training that year. Howard recalls the exchange:

"Skip, you wanted to see me?"

"Yeah, come in, come on in here, Bush." (Williams called everyone "Bush," for "Bush-Leaguer.")

"Can you tell me," Williams asked, "how a guy can hit 44 home runs but only get 48 base on balls?"

"Well, I try to be aggressive when I swing the bat," Howard responded.

"Yeah, yeah, yeah, I've seen you hit. You like that first swifty, that first little fastball you see," Williams said.

"Well, I better like that fastball, because that curveball, slider and changeup—to me they're UFOs,'" Howard said.

"What do you mean UFOs?" Williams asked.

"To me they're unidentifiable flying objects," Howard explained.

Williams finally managed a laugh.

"Did you ever take two strikes to get a good pitch to hit?" the new manager asked.

"God, Skip, if I took two strikes to get a good pitch to hit, I'd be walking back to the dugout 300 times a year instead of 125."

"Well, can you take a strike? I'm talking about a tough fastball, something other than what you're looking for, a curveball slider or change."

"Well, anybody can hit with a strike," Howard said.

"Well, try it for me," Williams asked.

The experiment was a success. Howard doubled his walk total from 48 to 102 that season, without sacrificing any power. He finished with his best season—a .296 average, 48 home runs, and 111 RBIs.

"If it was an identifiable pitch that I could really put a passable swing on, I'd let it fly," Howard says. "I started laying off a lot of the breaking balls off the plate in the dirt, and some of those borderline high fastballs that we swing through or foul back or pop up. It took an undisciplined hitter, who had a strike zone from the bill of his cap to his shoelaces, three or four inches in or off the plate, and tightened it up a bit.

"I found myself getting more hitter's counts—2–0, 3–1. He didn't mess much with guys mechanically if they'd play'd five or ten years in the big leagues, unless they'd had absolutely no success. But he sure messed with your coconut, your mental processes."

Short, ever the salesman, tried to capitalize on the buzz over the new manager, coining the marketing phrase, "It's a whole new ballgame." A then-Washington record opening-day crowd of 45,113, including President Nixon, showed up to see Williams in his managerial debut. Ted tipped his hat to the adoring fans during his introduction, something he hadn't done in his many years in Boston.

But some traditions die hard, and the Senators lost their seventh straight opener, falling to the New York Yankees, 8–4. Being a manager, Williams told reporters after the game, "felt lousy today," although he was impressed with the fans. "Really and truly, I think they're wonderful," he said. "They certainly got stirred up when we did a little something."

In July, Washington hosted its second All-Star Game in eight years. The city had hosted the 1962 contest to help christen its new state-of-the-art ballpark; now, Major League Baseball paid tribute to the nation's capital as part of the sport's 100th anniversary celebration. On the eve of the scheduled game, the Baseball Writers Association of America named its All-Time Team, voting Babe Ruth the greatest player ever, and former Senator Walter Johnson the greatest right-handed pitcher. Ted Williams was named to the all-time living team, but lost out to rival Joe DiMaggio as the greatest living player. Williams skipped the dinner, held at the Sheraton-Park Hotel.

The next day saw a rainout of the All-Star Game, the first time the game had been rained out in history. When the teams finally played the following afternoon, Howard gave Senators fans a chance to cheer for their hometown hero, smacking a 458-foot home run off Steve Carlton that landed over the clock in right-center field. They also booed the American League's starting shortstop, Boston's Rico Petrocelli, because they believed the rejuvenated Brinkman should have made the team.

Howard hit the longest homer, but the Giants' Willie McCovey hit the most. His two slams paced the National League's 9–3 victory. Howard also dropped a fly ball in the first inning, leading to the NL's first run.

Washington played around .500 ball most of the season, a huge improvement in its own right, but a late surge helped it finish 10 games over .500. The team won eight of its last nine games, including the season finale at RFK, which drew 18,000 fans, even though the Senators were well out of the pennant race.

"The fans were in a carnival mood, unwilling to let go of the most successful season in memory," wrote George Minot, Jr., in the *Post*. "They came to thank the Senators in general, and Ted Williams in particular, for bringing Washington back into the major leagues."

Williams's first year as manager was a success by any standard. He guided the team to an 86–76 record, the new Senators' first winning season and the best record for any Washington baseball team since 1945. The Senators had the sixth best record in the twelve-team league, but came in fourth place in the tough American League East.

Offense was up all across baseball because of the lowering of the pitching mound that season, but Williams's work with the Senators' hitters was phenomenal. The team's batting average jumped 27 points, to .251, and the Senators increased their home runs by 24 and walks by 174. In addition to Brinkman and Howard, several other players broke out offensively. Del Unser increased his batting average from .230 to .286; Mike Epstein had career highs in average (.278), home runs (30), and RBIs (85); and Ken McMullen increased his average from .248 to .272.

"Ted gave of himself to that ball club, and it's nice if you have an entire club have a career for you," recalls Howard. "And that's exactly what happened—we all had career years. As a result, we finished 10 games over .500. To be honest with you, we had a fine pitching staff, but if we'd had an ace on that staff, we might have taken them all on. We might have made a run at everybody."

Williams didn't mind taking his share of the credit. "They were all better hitters and not one son-of-a-bitch did I change his style," he said after the season.

Williams's work with the pitching staff was equally impressive. Despite the game's offensive thrust that year, the Senators' team ERA dropped from 3.64 to 3.49. Dick Bosman, who had gone 2–9 with a 3.69 ERA in 1968, improved to 14–5 under Williams with a league-best 2.19 ERA.

Bosman recalls Williams telling him in spring training of that year, "Boz, you got a chance to be pretty good. You just gotta learn to use what you got."

"When do we start?" Bosman asked.

"We already have," Williams replied.

Bosman said he became a disciple of the new manager.

"Ted and I had a relationship that a lot of guys didn't, and a lot of pitchers didn't," Bosman says. "Because, you know, Ted didn't like pitchers very well. And yet, we had a relationship that I would say, 90–95 percent of the time, that was very, very good. Ted believed that the slider was the toughest pitch to hit. I always threw a slider, and I made it better. He taught me that cat-and-mouse game about how to go back-and-forth between a breaking ball and a fastball. He taught me how to set up hitters. And basically, I learned how to use my breaking ball to set up my fastball."

Bosman says that Williams's excitement rubbed off on the players. "Ted Williams was enthusiastic," he says. "He was excited to be back in the game. He was big-time excited about being there, and we were too, because we were scuffling like ducks in the desert. We were bad. So to bring a guy in like that who was so excited about being there, shit, it was infectious man, it really was."

"He was very exuberant," recalls Brinkman. "He came in with a lot of pep. Chipper, ready for action."

That enthusiasm rubbed off of on the fans, too, 918,000 of whom came through the turnstiles, the best Washington attendance in 23 seasons, and the second highest in Senators history.

"Let me say that no one has been more enthusiastic than the 900,000 fucking fans," Williams told reporters after the final game.

Short, the new owner, wasn't satisfied. He told *Washington Post* sports columnist Bob Addie: "With the trade market we have in Washington, we should draw a million people." Back then, that was the gold standard for attendance. Short also complained about having to share the market with the Baltimore Orioles just 35 miles away, a complaint that the Orioles themselves would make many years later in an attempt to keep a team from returning to Washington.

"This is a great baseball area," Williams said after the season. "I can feel the enthusiasm mounting. I walk down the street and everyone tells me that we are doing a great job and that we're going to have a great year next year too."

Unfortunately, it didn't work out that way. The magic disappeared in 1970, and the Senators dropped to familiar territory—last place. In a foreshadowing of events, the team ended its spring training by playing two exhibition games in Arlington, Texas, on the way up to Washington. Nobody thought anything of it the time.

One highlight came on August 17, when Jim Hannan came close to throwing a no-hitter at RFK Stadium. With two outs in the fifth inning and the Senators leading the Royals, 7–0, Kansas City's Paul Schaal hit a line drive to left field. Frank Howard lunged for the ball and tried to make a shoestring catch, but came up a foot short. The ball raced past him and Schaal got a triple—the only hit Hannan would surrender that night in front of just 5,700 fans.

"Frank wore glasses, and it was a steamy night in Washington," Hannan recalls. "The lights at the time were a little bit low. He got a jump on the ball—he saw where it was coming—and he came in but he didn't really see the ball. He put his mitt in the wrong place, and it went to the fence for a triple, but the guy never scored, and that was the only hit. I understood, because I wore glasses, too, and I knew how they just steamed up and you just couldn't see."

Hannan's 7–0 one-hitter gave the Senators a seven-game winning streak, and the team's second one-hitter in five days (Bosman had one-hit the Twins the previous week). But the team stumbled after Hannan's game, losing the next three games to drop into last place.

Howard's performance on a September afternoon seemed to epitomize the team's frustrations. In the first game of a day-night doubleheader at Fenway Park, Howard struck out his first four times at bat. Howard's buddy, Brinkman, sat down next to the slugger in the dugout and asked, "You going to feature a little contact before this game is over?"

"And I told him zip it—he hadn't had a base hit in a month," Howard recalls with a laugh. "He's going to get all over me? So I said, 'Don't worry, Wimpy, just on get base in the ninth inning, and I'll pop one up in that net and we'll win a ballgame.' I figured I had this pitcher right in my gun sights to do just that."

Brinkman helped get Howard another at bat in the ninth inning by getting a base hit, and Howard came up with two outs and two runners on base. The Red Sox made a pitching change, bringing in a reliever who threw sliders and sinkers, the kinds of pitches that often gave Howard fits. The Washington slugger quickly fell behind with two quick strikes, and Brinkman, who was standing at second base, started taunting him, along with the Fenway fans, who were cheering for another strikeout.

"I'm trying to concentrate on this guy on the mound, and as I concentrate, here's my buddy at second base waving his hands, saying 'Five! You're going down again!'" Howard recalls. "The pitcher throws me another slider, and I strike out for the fifth straight time in a big league ball game. I wanted to kill Brinkman. He's running off the field laughing."

Boston fans jeered Howard: "I had 34,000 New Englanders all over me—'Go to work for a living, you clown!' I flipped them a bird and said, 'I love you too, you clam-eaters.' So I come out for the night game, and damn, if I don't fan my first time up. And that's six straight times. It's a record you don't want to set. I come up the seventh time and hit into a double play. I made eight outs in seven at bats, and got a standing ovation for it at Fenway Park."

Washington lost the first game, 7–3, and dropped the nightcap, 11–3, making four errors in the second game alone.

Howard's propensity for strikeouts earned him some ribbing from his own manager, too. One of Howard's legacies at RFK is the white-painted seats in the upper deck of the stadium, to mark where his monstrous home runs landed. A friend of Ted Williams saw the seats before one game and asked, "Geez, is that where Howard hit those long home runs?"

Williams responded: "Yeah, and there's 13,980 green seats up there—those are all the times he struck out on me."

Still, Howard had a great year in 1970, despite the performance at Fenway Park. He led the league in home runs (44), RBIs (126), and walks (132), and hit a team-best .283. But 1970 was a disaster for the Senators as a whole, especially coming off such a successful season the year before. Washington finished the season with a crushing 14 straight losses.

Short pulled off a blockbuster trade a couple of weeks later, sending his left side of the infield—shortstop Brinkman and third baseman Aurelio Rodriguez—to the Detroit Tigers for talented but troubled pitcher Denny McLain in an eight-player deal. Rodriguez had been acquired by Washington just six months earlier, and put up decent numbers in 1970, batting .247 with 19 home runs and 76 RBIs. Brinkman, an excellent defensive shortstop, was coming off his second straight successful offensive year, batting .262. Washington also parted with pitchers Hannan and Joe Coleman, and received from Detroit third baseman Don Wert, outfielder-third baseman Elliott Maddox, and pitcher Norm McRae.

McLain, only 25, had been one of the game's dominant pitchers, winning 31 games in 1968 en route to the Cy Young award, and going 24–9 in 1969. But he missed much of the 1970 season because of disciplinary problems. Commissioner Bowie Kuhn suspended him for half the year for associating with bookmakers; the team's general manager yanked him for four days after McLain dumped ice water on a couple of sportswriters; and on September 9, the commissioner removed him for the remainder of the season over allegations that the pitcher had carried a gun. Overall, McLain went 3–5 in the shortened year.

Short, who also picked up $200,000 in the trade, conceded that Ted Williams was not happy with the deal. "He thinks the price Detroit extracted was too high—although Ted feels he can handle McLain." Short's real motivation, besides the cash, was getting more fans into the stadium; Washington's attendance had fallen to 824,000 in 1970, a drop-off of about 90,000 from the previous season. He said McLain would "improve the gate" at RFK.

In an early warning about the fate of the team, Short was also beginning to make some noise about improving the lease deal at the stadium. He wanted free rent on the first million fans; parking revenue (of which he received none); and all of the concessions revenue, instead of the sliding-scale percentage he was getting. He argued that the increased revenue would allow him to spend money to improve the team.

"If I don't get what I want, I will declare bankruptcy," he said, but added, "If I don't get what I want, the American League will operate the club in Washington. I will not request a move."

Four days after the trade, Short testified at a House District Committee hearing to make his case for a better lease on the stadium.

"I am not trying to get rent free," he said. "I am trying to get someone who runs that building to recognize . . . we don't have the money to police it. We don't have the money to put in the infield and to maintain it. We don't have the money to pay a minimum rental." The lease, which expired at the end of the '71 season, called for the Senators to pay $65,000 or 7 percent of gross ticket receipts, whichever was greater.

In November 1970, Short acquired outfielder Curt Flood from the Philadelphia Phillies for three minor leaguers. Flood had unsuccessfully challenged baseball's reserve clause—refusing a trade in 1969 from the St. Louis Cardinals to the Philadelphia Phillies—and sat out the entire 1970 season. This deal, too, was made with increasing attendance in mind. Short said he lost $953,000 in 1970.

"We need great players and these guys are controversial," Short told the *Post*. "With McLain pitching, even if we have a bad team, they'll come to see him because he's a face. Ted Williams is a face. Flood is a face. Frank Howard is a face. Without Frank Howard last season, we wouldn't have drawn flies."

Short's money problems, however, were more tied to his own financing of the team than attendance or lease conditions. More than $700,000 of his operating losses came from interest he paid on loans he took out to buy the team.

His poverty cries got a skeptical response from the media, especially because the Senators charged the highest ticket prices in the league.

"If Short needs money so badly, (fans) might ask, why doesn't he sell his jet plane or at least put it in mothballs until his financial crisis is resolved?" Minot wrote. "He uses the Lear jet the way the rest of us use a taxi."

Starting out on a hopeful note, the Senators finally snapped two losing streaks on April 5, 1971. One was the 14-game skid that marked the end of the 1970 season. The other was the opening-day drought dating back to 1963. After eight straight opening-day losses, the Senators finally gave their hometown fans a win in the American League's traditional opener. Unfortunately, it would be the last opening day in Washington Senators history.

Bosman threw a six-hit shutout in the 8–0 victory over the Oakland Athletics, as the Senators beat Vida Blue, who went on to win the Cy Young Award that year. Rookie Toby Harrah, the Senators' new shortstop, got two hits and scored two runs. The team even got off to a 12–8 start, a .600 winning percentage.

But the famous veterans Short had brought in were not working out. Flood quit the team in late April, after playing 13 games in Washington. He retired with a lifetime .293 average, but hit just .200 in his one month with the Senators. Similarly, McLain never regained his pitching form, and was also plagued by poor run support. He became a 20-game loser (10–22, 4.28 ERA) three years after becoming baseball's last 30-game winner.

But the Senators had bigger troubles than their on-the-field performance. In June, the D.C. Armory Board sent letters to Commissioner Bowie Kuhn and American League President Joe Cronin, informing them that Short was $161,000 behind in rent. The board, complaining that Short had not responded to letters and requests for meetings, said it could take several actions against Short, including turning out the stadium lights and locking the gates if rent wasn't received by July 15. Kuhn called a meeting of the 12 American League owners, who authorized Cronin to try to find a solution. After the eight-hour meeting, Short said that he had not sought permission to move the team to Dallas, as had been rumored.

"I never wanted to, I never intended to, but that doesn't mean I won't move," he told the *Post*.

Meanwhile, Short denied having polled the other owners to see if he had the required support of nine of the twelve league owners to move the team. "I don't think it will ever come to that," he said. On July 7, Kuhn, Cronin, and Short met with Armory Board officials, who agreed not to shut off the lights on July 15 and to look into what concessions could have been made to alleviate Short's financial woes.

In an effort to keep the team in Washington, the board made an offer to Short for the 1972 season. As the owner had demanded, the team would pay no rent on the first million fans; after that, revenue would be split equally between the Senators and the board. The Senators would also get food and beverage profits during the baseball season. But the board would not agree to give Short the parking revenue he had sought. Overall, the board said, Short would save about $125,000 a year under the deal.

Short called the offer a step in the right direction, "but kind of late."

As the team began its final weeks in Washington, several groups came forward to try to save the Senators. Bob Hope, who had lost his bid to buy the team in 1968, offered Short $7.45 million, but was rejected. Short, who had paid $9.4 million, wanted $12 million for the team, arguing he needed the profit to offset $3 million in operating losses.

Joseph B. Danzansky, president of both Giant Food Stores and the Washington Board of Trade, said he would pay $8 million for the team. Bill Veeck and former Tigers slugger Hank Greenberg, who had been partners in the Chicago White Sox ownership, also made a last-ditch effort to buy the team and prevent it from moving.

Short must have been surprised that he wasn't getting better offers. Back in 1969, he told Al Eisele for a *Washingtonian* profile, "The team now probably isn't worth what I paid for it, but nobody ever lost money selling a big-league baseball franchise. Even if I mismanage the team, it will still be worth close to what I paid for it."

Meanwhile, a contingent from Texas was trying to lasso the team. The mayors of Dallas, Fort Worth, and Arlington presented a unified front for a team in Arlington, which was located equally between the other two cities. Texas banks offered Short a $7.5 million line of credit at low interest.

Just days before a vote by American League owners to settle the fate of the Senators, the major players were still publicly stating that the team would likely stay in Washington. Commissioner Kuhn said he'd be surprised if Short sought permission to move, and on the eve of the vote, Short told the *Post* that someone would buy the team and keep it in the nation's capital.

"I don't think the District of Columbia will allow it to move," he said, adding that he didn't think he would ask permission to move the team.

But Short did ask permission to move—and on September 21, 1971, at a meeting in Boston, the American League owners voted 10–2 to allow him to do so. Danzansky made a final offer to buy the team, but the owners concluded that the financing was too thin. The only teams to vote against the move were the Chicago White Sox and, ironically, the Baltimore Orioles. Decades later, the Orioles would fight vociferously to keep a team from returning to Washington.

Kuhn says that Baltimore's vote against letting the Senators move was just for show.

"They didn't want to make Washington fans unhappy," he says now, recalling the vote. "They knew good and well how the vote was going to go."

Although the Orioles were against letting the team move, their owner immediately made clear that now that Washington was without a team, the city was Baltimore territory. *Washington Post* sports editor Shirley Povich reported that after the vote, Orioles owner Jerold Hoffberger told his fellow owners: "Gentlemen, this means the Orioles now control all territory within one hundred miles of Baltimore under the American League rules, and I will veto any shift of another league franchise to Washington."

Hours before the vote, the Senators played in front of just 1,072 fans in a game against Cleveland, reinforcing the funereal atmosphere of the stadium. Only four games remained after that.

The Senators moved on the watch of a league president and commissioner with strong historical ties to Washington baseball. Cronin had been a popular player for the Senators in the 1920s and '30s, leading the team to its last pennant as player-manager in 1933. He was even part of owner Clark Griffith's family, marrying Griffith's niece and adopted daughter, Mildred Robertson.

"As an old Washington player, this is very sad, indeed, but there was no feasible alternative," Cronin said when making the announcement at 11:30 p.m.

Kuhn grew up in Washington and operated the scoreboard at old Griffith Stadium as a youth. "It is a sad day after the better part of a century in Washington," Kuhn said. "But it's a great day for Dallas-Fort Worth, which everyone agrees is ready for major league baseball."

Reflecting on the meeting decades later, Kuhn says, "It was terrible. It was the only time I ever cried as commissioner. I did everything I could to save it. I held it up for months. Finally, we had the American League meeting. I couldn't make an argument against it. I stood there with tears down my face."

Richard M. Nixon, the last in a line of 20th-century presidents to throw out a first ball at the traditional presidential opener, said he was "distressed" by the news, and would now switch his allegiance to the California Angels, who were based near his home of San Clemente, California. The Angels, coincidentally, had entered the American League with the Senators in 1961.

Ted Williams said he encouraged Red Sox owner Tom Yawkey to approve the move.

"The American League people would have been crazy if they hadn't allowed the shift," he said. "The way things are set up in this town—bad rent, bad concessions, no television market—hell, nobody could make it. There was a hard core of fans here all right, but there were only six or seven thousand of them. Basically Washington is a city of transient people. Most people don't give a damn."

Unlike the last team move in 1961, this time there was no expansion team waiting in the on-deck circle to take the Senators' place. That meant an end to major league baseball in Washington after 71 years, three pennants, and one World Series championship.

"I face you all in failure because I was not able to do what I wanted to do," Short told reporters. "I worked with diligence with Mr. Kuhn and Mr. Cronin to find a solution to the problem." He said the Texas deal offered him "more favorable terms than any baseball operator I know of," such as a one-dollar-a-year rent on the first million fans, a share of parking and concession revenue, and a radio-TV contract valued at $1 million a year—double what Short had gotten in broadcasting revenue in D.C.

The Senators were moving from RFK Stadium to the inelegantly named Turnpike Stadium, located on a toll road halfway between Dallas and Fort Worth. But it would take some time for the transplanted team, renamed the Rangers, to catch on in Texas. They drew 663,000 in 1972, just 8,000 more than the Senators' last lame-duck season in Washington.

"Baseball is a business, as far as Mr. Short is concerned," the *Washington Post* editorialized, "and his devotion to the idea of keeping baseball alive in the nation's capital was, to be generous about it, wafer-thin. . . . So we say goodbye to Mr. Short with hardly a tear, while wishing the Senators well in their new Texas home. Fans there, inexperienced with the ways of baseball promoters, may be eager for a while to pay big league prices to see minor league ball and get free who-knows-what."

A *Washington Star* editorial also criticized Short's reliance on giveaways, such as Hot Pants Day and pantyhose night: "Bob Short was not worthy of us. He spent too much, cared too little, and thought he could buy his way out of his mistakes with high-priced tickets and pantyhose. Let him go. To hell with it. And yet . . . "

Fans took the news hard. Bill Gilbert, the team's former marketing director, described in a letter to the editor telling his seven-year-old son the news: "The blond head immediately buried itself in the pillow on his bed, face down. He was crying. After an eternity, the head struggled its way up from the pillow. . . . He said, 'I'll never see Frank Howard ever again.'"

One fan suggested a new name for the team: "The Dallas-Fort Worthless Senators."

Phil Hochberg, a lifelong Senators fan who served as the team's public address announcer from 1962 to 1968, says the move was crushing.

"I was 30 years old, and this was as close to a feeling as somebody in my family dying as I have ever had—certainly up to that time," Hochberg recalls. "A feeling of total helplessness. You can see it happening and there's nothing you can do about it. I guess it's all of the emotions that one feels when a loved one dies. Maybe I ought to grow up, but this was an important part of my life, and Bob Short took it away from me. And he didn't have the right to take it away from me. From the time I was seven years old, this was an important part of my life."

The Senators became the fourth team to move in six years. The Milwaukee Braves had moved to Atlanta in 1966; the Kansas City Athletics had relocated to Oakland in 1968; and the Seattle Pilots had left for Milwaukee in 1970, after just one season on the West Coast. With all of the team shifts, Washington baseball boosters were confident they could land a new team. After all, the three cities that had lost teams in the '60s would land replacement clubs within a few years. But the era of franchise moves ended with the Senators.

Washington officials didn't waste any time in trying to get a new team. Mayor Walter Washington named Danzansky to make a pitch to the San Diego Padres, who were struggling to draw fans in only their third year. But nothing came of it. The Padres had entered the National League in 1969, along with the Montreal Expos—the team Washington would finally land 34 years later.

On September 30, the same date the Washington Senators had clinched their first pennant 47 years earlier, the team suited up for its last game ever, against the New York Yankees. Some 14,460 fans, nearly double the average crowd that season, showed up for the last rites. Four thousand more slipped through unmanned turnstiles as the game went on, wrote Jeff Stuart in his revealing book, *Twilight Teams*. Like a family trying to unload its unwanted stuff before moving out of a house, the Senators gave away leftover promotional materials, such as balls, caps, shirts, and copies of Williams's book, *My Turn at Bat*.

The crowd was festive and sad, trying to celebrate its one last game while pouring out its acrimony toward Short. "To those among the crowd who had come in sorrow," wrote Povich the next day, "the Star Spangled Banner never before sounded so much like a dirge." To the city's embittered fans, he added, Arlington, Texas, "is some jerk town with the single boast it is equidistant from Dallas and Fort Worth."

Before the game, a couple of fans went on top of the dugout with a sign that read, "How Dare You Sell Us Short." During the game, two long, skinny signs were unfurled from the left-field stands next to each other, with vertical letters spelling out "Short" and "Stinks," prompting a standing ovation. One fan wore a black mourning arm band. At one point, fans started chanting "We Want Bob Short."

The owner, of course, was nowhere near the place. But he did call the radio station that was airing the game, to complain about announcer Ron Menchine, who was criticizing Short throughout the broadcast.

In the sixth inning, Howard gave the fans their final thrill, blasting a home run off the back of the Yankees bullpen, as part of a four-run rally that tied the score. The fan-favorite waved his batting helmet in the air, tossed his cap into the stands, and blew kisses to the fans. He also told Yankees catcher Thurmon Munson as he crossed the plate, "Thanks for the gift." Pitcher Mike Kekich suggested he grooved one to Howard. "It's OK," he said. "Let's just say I tried to throw him a straight pitch."

"This is utopia," Howard said after the game. "This is the greatest thrill of my life. What would top it?"

Even now, decades later, Howard says, "It sends chills through your spine, makes your hair stand on edge. You're playing in front of your people, and you want to satisfy them. It was a very emotional highlight in my career."

At the beginning of the eighth inning, some fans started coming on the field, but order was restored. Williams, sensing pandemonium, lifted Howard from the game. In the top of the ninth inning, fans again raced onto the field, prompting a warning from the public address announcer that the game could be forfeited.

Joe Grzenda took the mound in the bottom of the ninth with the Senators leading, 7–5. Grzenda had been one of the Senators' few highlights that year, going 5–2 with a 1.92 ERA for a fifth-place team that finished 63–96, its worst record in seven years. Grzenda recalls how he had instructions to hesitate after getting the second out of the inning, to give the bullpens a chance to empty out.

"Because they knew something was going to happen," he says. "They were rowdy going back to the fourth inning. After I got two outs, Horace Clarke came up. I wasted some time, kicking dirt around, and Horace stood in that batting circle taking those practice swings. And I yelled, 'C'mon let's go!' I looked around, and it was over. They came over the fence, and there was actually dust flying. There were hundreds that came over the fence. It looked like a heard of cattle coming in those old movies, when they stampede."

Still, Grzenda says, he wasn't scared. "The fans they had in Washington were all good fans. They wouldn't hurt us. I think when Frank Howard went into the dugout, two kids jumped on his back. And when he went down, he just brushed them off with the roof of the dugout."

Tom McCaw, who would become the Washington Nationals' first batting coach in 2005, was on the field as the Senators' first baseman for that final game. He recalls seeing what looked like confetti blowing around RFK in the sixth inning of that final game.

"By the seventh inning, it got worse, then you could recognize what it was—it was part of Ted Williams's book that they were tearing up," he says. "I was playing first base, and the umpire said to me, 'Mack, they're coming out on this field, and I'm going to get out of here.' And I said, 'Well if you leave, I will be in your back pocket.' And sure enough about the eighth inning, two or three guys came on the field, and it turned into eight, nine, and ten, and then they just kind of swarmed the field in the ninth inning. And hell, he took up, and true to my word, I went right with him. I just went in the clubhouse and waited for a couple of hours."

The final game in Washington Senators history was recorded as a forfeit, as play was never restored. Fans pulled up bases, numbers from the scoreboard, light bulbs, chunks of grass. The final score was 9–0, the traditional forfeit score in baseball. But all the records, including Howard's home run, counted.

POSTSCRIPT

The team continued its downward trajectory in its first year in Texas. The Rangers finished 54–100 in 1972, a .351 winning percentage, the worst record in the major leagues. Ted Williams quit after the season, and was replaced the next year by Whitey Herzog. The 1973 Rangers finished with a nearly identical winning percentage of .352, again last in the majors. Billy Martin took over the team at the end of the year, and led the team to a second-place finish in 1974. The Rangers have yet to win a pennant in Texas, although they did win three division titles in the 1990s.

Meanwhile, a few hardcore Senators fans made it their life's mission to get revenge on Bob Short in the years after the move. Bill Holdforth, who had worked as an usher at RFK, recalls circling the date when the old Senators would be returning to the area for a game against the Baltimore Orioles.

"When we saw the 1972 schedule and saw when Texas would be coming to Baltimore, we said, we would be at that game and we were going to do something," recalls Holdforth, who is known as "Baseball Bill."

"We decided we had to take an effigy with us. My brother Bob helped me stuff it with old *Sporting News*, back when it was a newspaper. We added a shirt and tie. And we put a sign on the front, 'Short Stinks,' got in the car and went up to Baltimore."

Holdforth and his buddies got tickets in Short's section and laid the effigy under their seats. Then Holdforth approached an usher he knew, and said, "I don't know when, but sometime during the game, we're going to take the dummy down and stand right by Short. We're just going down to taunt him. We don't want to get thrown out, and we don't want to get you in trouble, so when you want us to leave, we'll make you look good, we'll go right back."

Newspaper photos the next day showed the husky, 21-year-old Holdforth grinning mischievously as he holds the effigy behind Short, who is wearing an exasperated expression. Holdforth's buddy stands behind the effigy holding a sign that reads, "Short stinks."

"I stood over Short for two or three minutes. He looked very uncomfortable," Holdforth recalls, still laughing about it decades later. "And we said, 'What's the matter, Bobby Baby? Is something bothering you?' He turned around and said, 'Why don't you go fuck yourself?' I just busted out laughing. When you get a response like that, then you know you're being effective."

In Washington baseball lore, Holdforth is also the guy credited with dumping beer on Short, but Holdforth insists that part of the story isn't true. An inning later, Holdforth says, he went to the bathroom, and when he came out, fans were in a tizzy over a woman who poured a beer on the Rangers owner.

"I wouldn't waste a beer like that," says Holdforth, who worked for several years at the Capitol Hill bar, Hawk 'n' Dove.

Holdforth and his friends continued their crusade even after Short sold the Rangers and tried to get back into politics. In 1978, Short ran for U.S. Senate as a Democrat from his home state of Minnesota, and the group formed "Baseball Bill's Committee to Keep Bob Short out of D.C." to try to defeat him. The still-seething Senators fans raised $3,500 in a backyard fundraiser, and used the money to take out a half-page ad in the *Minneapolis Star* the Sunday before the Democratic primary.

"Don't Be 'SHORT' Changed," the ad read. "Bob Short WAS a Senator. In fact, he was the Washington Senators, the American League Baseball Club. He purchased the team in December 1968. He moved the team to Arlington, Texas at the end of September 1971. We in our Nation's Capital were left without a baseball team. We were 'short changed.' In two days you people of the great state of Minnesota must make a decision. Bob Short held our trust for three years and we were SHORT CHANGED. So, before you vote Tuesday, please consider these facts about Bob Short as we know him."

The ad then lists several comments Short made, contrasted with his actions that led to the team being moved.

"Seventy-one years of baseball tradition meant nothing to him. Minnesotans have a tradition of sending men of national stature like Humphrey, Mondale and McCarthy to the U.S. Senate. Does Bob Short's record measure up? We think not."

And then the kicker: "P.S. you can keep Cal Griffith, too," who had moved the first Senators team to Minnesota in 1961.

Short won the Democratic primary anyway, and the group figured that was that. But a week later, Holdforth says, they got a call from the campaign of the Republican candidate, Dave Durenberger, asking for permission to make copies of the ad and distribute them at Minnesota Vikings football games.

"So we said sure," Holdforth recalls. "We made it clear, we wanted to see Short lose." Durenberger wound up defeating Short, and the senator-elect paid a visit to the group after the election.

"I remember he was just one of those guys that I had to go meet," recalls Durenberger. "I wanted to go see my buddy, Baseball Billy! When I met him, I thought wow, how can you miss this guy? He's really a larger-than-life character. I'd never seen a bartender quite that big. He didn't make any bones about it—was he a big David Durenberger supporter? No. His goal was to keep Short out of Washington, D.C. And he was happy that I was available to do it."

Durenberger thinks the Holdforth effort helped.

"The campaign was taking advantage of every anti-Short thing they could take advantage of," he says. "The guy had a lot of negatives, and they wanted to increase it—so Baseball Billy was one way to do it. It was an easy of way of saying, folks in Washington don't want Bob Short any more than people in Minnesota want him."

Washington would continue its quest for a team for more than three decades after the Senators left for Texas. In 1974, the city was so close to landing the Padres that Topps printed baseball cards of Padres players with "Washington" written on them. The deal fell through when McDonald's founder Ray A. Kroc bought the team and kept it in San Diego. In 1977, the National League passed on a chance to expand to Washington, deciding to stay put with 12 teams as the American League expanded to Toronto and Seattle.

Subsequent expansions in 1993 and 1998 also bypassed the nation's capital. In 2001, Major League Baseball tried unsuccessfully to eliminate two teams. One was the Minnesota Twins, the original Washington Senators franchise. The other was the Montreal Expos, the team that would become the new Washington Nationals.

When baseball finally moved the Expos to Washington for the 2005 season, it marked a historical accounting with the city of Montreal. Calvin Griffith, the man who relocated the original Senators to Minnesota, was a Montreal native.

NINE

FANS, MOMENTS, AND MEMORIES

NINE

FANS, MOMENTS, AND MEMORIES

An old expression about the Senators, "First in war, first in peace, and last in the American League," aptly described Washington baseball's final quarter-century, from the end of World War II through 1971. But a sportswriter named Charles Dryden had actually coined the phrase back in the team's early 1900s infancy, making a play on Henry Lee's eulogy to George Washington: "First in war, first in peace and first in the hearts of his countrymen."

The Washington Nationals—popularly known as the Senators—started off with 11 straight losing seasons. Clark Griffith reversed the team's fortunes when he took over as manager in 1912, leading the team to a strong second-place finish, and Washington actually posted good teams, on and off, through the early 1930s.

But for many Washingtonians, losing was an intrinsic part of being a Senators fan. In 1954, native Washingtonian Douglass Wallop penned *The Year the Yankees Lost the Pennant*, about a middle-aged Senators fan who sells his soul to the Devil in return for being transformed into the young slugger Joe Hardy, who helps the Senators win the pennant. *Damn Yankees*, the musical based on the novel, opened to rave reviews on Broadway in 1955. In real life, the Senators finished in last place that year, 38 games behind the first-place Yankees. It was but small comfort to Senators fans when the hated Yankees lost the World Series that year to the Brooklyn Dodgers.

Washington fans were not exactly coming out in droves at the time. The Senators drew just 425,000 in 1955, an average of 5,500 fans a game. In the years before luxury boxes, going to a Senators game was for the hardcore fans only.

"There wasn't a lot of passion for the Senators," recalls Phil Hochberg, who was a young Nats fan at the time and went on to become the Senators' public address announcer in the 1960s. "The fans who were there were passionate, but there were so few. They had been beaten down by so many losing teams for so many years. Between 1946 and 1971—that's 26 years—they finished over .500 twice. That's abysmal! So there wasn't any enthusiasm."

Hochberg said that by the 1950s, Griffith Stadium was not a particularly friendly place to watch a game. The park sat at the corner of 7th Street and Florida Avenue, Northwest, near Howard University.

"There was no parking to speak of, so you had to park on the street," Hochberg says. "So little kids would come by and say, 'I'll watch your car, Mister, for twenty-five cents.' And if you didn't give them the twenty-five cents, there was no telling what would happen to your car. Griffith Stadium was an old ballpark, it had lots of character, but it was not a particularly good place to watch a ballgame from. You had obstructed seats. You had girders holding up the right-field stands, and you couldn't see the left-field stands. There was nothing wonderful about Griffith Stadium except that it was a baseball stadium."

Joe Dempsey, who went to ballgames in the 1950s, remembers the sounds of the old ballpark: "Get yer' red hots, hare! Get 'em while 'air hot. . . . Col' be-ah, get cher' col' be-ah." One vendor in particular stands out in Dempsey's memory: "In a high-pitched, somewhat raspy voice came a slow drawn-out but very clear 'It is NOW time to EAT, DRINK and be MERRY! Get yo' Hot dawgs, he-ah!'"

"Griffith Stadium was an old rickety, run down stadium," says Dempsey, now a real estate agent in Warrenton, Virginia. "The girders and beams reminded me of my Erector Set at home. As you entered the seating area, everything was painted dark green and the emerald lawn of the playing field seemed to jump at you. The sound of the gathering crowds was muffled and the crack of the ball and bat of batting practice was pronounced."

But some fans thought the old ballpark had charm.

"The right-field wall was a favorite of mine," says Jack Farley, who started going to games in the 1930s. "The scoreboard was attached to it and someone would go inside the wall and hang signs for the runs scored by each team during each inning. Once in a while, the person would drop a sign and it would fall on the playing field. Then he would come out of a little door and pick up the sign. The crowd loved it."

Manning the scoreboard in the 1940s was Bowie Kuhn, a Washington native who later became baseball commissioner.

"It was one of the best jobs I ever had," says Kuhn, who held the job as a teenager, before joining the Navy. "The scoreboard was in right-center, and it looked out on an alley through a window. There was always a bunch of kids in the alley who I would talk to. I got in the habit of doing play-by-play for the kids, who couldn't see into the ballpark."

"It was a wonderful old stadium," Kuhn adds. "The sightlines were good, as long as you didn't get behind pillars. The pavilion seats were 60 cents, where all the old-time fans would bet on the game. The bleachers were 40 cents."

Farley, who is retired in Rehoboth Beach, Delaware, recalls even better specials. "Mom would take me to Ladies Day games where she got in for 25 cents and I got in for free. Once we got there, there would be the wonderful smell of the Wonder Bread Bakery next door baking bread, which would waft into the bleachers."

You also didn't have to pay four bucks for a bottle of water back then—or anything, for that matter. In the summer of 1941, baseball fans were shocked about reports that ushers were charging fans a dime for a glass of ice water.

Owner Clark Griffith originally denied this scandalous accusation, which appeared in a New York newspaper called *PM*.

But after investigating, Griffith issued the following statement: "I find proof that some concession boys, particularly in the bleachers, took advantage of the big crowd on the 29th of June to make themselves a little easy money by selling ice water. The Washington club deeply regrets that such a thing could have happened and wants to apologize to the Washington public and assure them that it will not occur again. In fact, this is the first time in thirty years that anything like this has happened. The boys involved in this circumstance will be discharged."

Griffith made a point of making the place a family-friendly environment. He refused to sell beer at the stadium, but he did sell advertising space to beer companies.

Although there was no Metro and little parking, fans did have another way of getting to the games: the streetcar.

"One time, on the way to the game, we saw Buddy Lewis standing in the back of our street car," Farley recalls, referring to the Senators' All-Star third baseman. "Buddy rented an upstairs single room from one of our neighbors during the season."

Farley grew up near Catholic University, and would take the streetcar to North Capital Street. From there, he'd walk five blocks to the 5th Street bleacher entrance.

"I went to many games alone at night," he recalls. "I used to leave many of the games early since the team was usually pretty far behind. I used to walk past the small row houses occupied by poor blacks. They would sit on their little step at night trying to cool off."

Some young fans relied on the players themselves for transportation. Henry Fankhauser, who later became a sportswriter for the old *Washington Daily News*, says he and his friends would wait outside the Senators' clubhouse and ask the players for rides home.

"We'd follow them out to the parking lot, and ask them for autographs, and say, 'By the way, we live in your neighborhood, can we get a ride?'" Fankhauser recalls.

Bill Gilbert remembers waiting after a game in 1944 for outfielder George Case, who lived in his neighborhood. But when Shirley Povich, who covered the team for the *Washington Post*, came out, he informed the youngster that Case had already left. So Povich, who also lived near Gilbert, not only gave him a ride home, he offered to take him to the ballpark anytime.

"So the next morning, I called and said, 'I'd like a ride to the game,'" Gilbert recalls. "I brought a hundred and ten pennies to pay the $1.10 general admission fee. When we got out of the car, he brought me up to the press gate, and said to the attendant, 'He's with me.' He probably took me to 35 games."

The next year, 1945, Gilbert and Fankhauser rode their bikes to spring training at College Park, Maryland (a World War II ban on unnecessary travel prevented teams from going south to train). Gilbert, 13, got a job as team batboy. There he met one of the most unusual players in Washington baseball history: Bert Shepard.

Shepard, a fighter pilot who had his left leg amputated under his knee, wound up at Walter Reed Hospital for an artificial limb. While there, he received a visit from Undersecretary of War Robert Patterson, who asked Shepard what he wanted to do after the war. The former minor league pitcher said he wanted to pitch again.

Patterson called Griffith and asked if he'd give Shepard a tryout. The Senators owner agreed, and after Shepard held his own in the 1945 tryout, the team signed him as a player-coach.

"In the dressing room I would watch as he would strap his artificial leg on before the workout and take it off after and hop on one foot into the shower," Gilbert wrote years later.

Shepard pitched in an exhibition game that season, on July 10, and held the Brooklyn Dodgers to two runs in four innings. On August 4, he finally pitched in an official game. In the midst of a blowout at the hands of the Boston Red Sox, Shepard was summoned from the bullpen at Griffith Stadium to help give the pitching staff a breather—the team was playing its fourth doubleheader in four days, with another one scheduled for the next day.

Shepard came into the game with two outs in the fourth inning and the bases loaded. Striding and landing on his artificial limb, he struck out George "Catfish" Metkovich to end the rally, and received a standing ovation. Shepard pitched the rest of way, giving up just one run and three hits in a total of 5⅓ innings. That was his first and last performance in a big league game. His lifetime ERA stands at 1.69.

The Senators' original stadium, known as the American League Base Ball Park, was constructed of wood, but after a 1911 fire, the team rebuilt it with steel and concrete. Authorities suspected the fire had been started by a plumber's blowtorch, prompting the team's former manager, Joe Cantillion, to quip: "They're probably right, and the plumber was probably playing third base." The ballpark was renamed Griffith Stadium in 1920 for its owner.

Griffith Stadium was definitely not a hitter's ballpark. Although the dimensions changed throughout the years, it was usually a monstrous 400 feet or more down the left-field line, longer than any major league ballpark today. The right-field line, by contrast, was usually around 328 feet, but hitters had to clear a 30-foot-high fence, a kind of mirror-image Green Monster. The fence in center field cut a sharp turn toward home plate to avoid a large oak tree just outside the ballpark, a popular meeting spot for fans. Both Mickey Mantle and Babe Ruth hit balls into the tree.

No ballpark could hold the Mick. In 1953, his home run shot glanced off the National Bohemian Beer sign on top of the bleachers in left-center field, on its way out of the stadium into someone's backyard. The ball traveled 565 feet, the longest measured home run in major league history.

After the game, a sportswriter suggested that the wind was blowing out, to which Clark Griffith retorted, "Consarn it, that same wind has been blowing for a hundred years, and nobody else ever hit one over that wall."

But the Senators lacked that kind of power, wind or not. The stadium was so unfriendly to the home team's sluggers that in 1945, the Senators went the entire season without hitting a ball over the fence. Washington's sole home run that year came on an inside-the-parker by first baseman Joe Kuhel. And this was one of Washington's best teams—the Senators finished just 1½ games out of first place.

"I was a dead-pull hitter, and it was 405 feet to left field," recalls Eddie Yost, a third baseman who played for the Senators in the 1940s and '50s. "Once, I hit 12 home runs in back-to-back seasons, and only one of them came at Griffith Stadium." Yost never hit more than a dozen home runs in any of his dozen seasons in Washington. After the Senators traded him to Detroit, he hit 21 his first season with the Tigers.

Yost made up for a lack of home-field power with an uncanny ability to draw walks. He led the league in bases on balls six times, including a career-high 151 in 1956, earning him the nickname "The Walking Man." Yost was a respected player back in his day. But in today's game, which cherishes on-base percentage, he would be a celebrity. Although he hit only .254 for his career, he finished with a high .394 on-base percentage.

Griffith Stadium may have been hostile to home runs, but with its vast distances and strange angles, it was friendly to triples. In the 51 seasons the team played at the ballpark after it was rebuilt in 1911, the Senators led or tied for the league lead in three-baggers 17 times—including seven times in the 1930s alone.

When Calvin Griffith took over the team in 1955 after the death of Clark Griffith, the new president moved the fences in about 30 feet all around. He also scrapped the Old Fox's ban on alcohol and opened a beer garden in the left-field seats.

"We did it for revenue," Calvin Griffith told biographer Jon Kerr. "We wanted to sell beer out there to stay in baseball. We had to do something different."

Mickey Mantle wrote about the beer garden fondly in his book, *The Mick*: "There were so many good fights in the left field bleachers in the beer garden—or women sunbathing about naked—that several times I was watching that when I'd hear the crack of the bat and I'd have to spin around to see which direction everybody was runnin.'"

The ballpark's seating capacity, which also varied through the years, was never more than around 32,000. But the Griffith family supplemented income from the park by renting it out to the Homestead Grays of the Negro Leagues during the baseball season, and to the Washington Redskins during football season. Griffith Stadium hosted the most one-sided game in NFL history, when the Chicago Bears beat the Redskins, 73–0, to win the 1940 championship game.

When the Senators were away, their fans could still follow the action—with a little embellishment from Hall-of-Fame radio broadcaster Arch McDonald.

"Back in those days there was no television and one had to listen to the games on the radio," recalls Robert G. Hardage of Fairfax, Virginia, who started following the Nationals in the 1940s. "The budget was so tight that the announcers did not travel to away games with the team but had to re-create the contest after receiving a teletype wire about what had transpired.

"For away games, one could hear the teletype in the background as you waited to find out what had occurred," says Hardage, a retired high school football coach and athletic director. "Arch McDonald's trademark was a bell or 'gong' for a base hit. A double was two gongs and naturally a home run was four gongs but generally proceeded by the comment from Arch, 'There she goes, Mrs. Murphy.'"

McDonald would recreate the games from the Peoples Drug Store on G Street, a few blocks from the White House, where he would draw overflow crowds, earning him the nickname the "Rembrandt of Recreation." The Arkansas native coined popular baseball phrases such as "ducks on the pond" and "right down Broadway," and even came up with the nickname for Joe DiMaggio, "The Yankee Clipper." McDonald announced Senators games for 22 years, with a one-year break in 1939 to broadcast Yankee games. "They cut down the old pine tree," he'd say after a Senators victory, quoting from an old country song.

Attendance at Griffith Stadium started to tank in the 1950s, thanks to consistently bad teams. In 1956, Washington hired Charlie Brotman as promotions director, and he tried to generate some excitement at the ballpark. One of his first moves: a simple name change—to what fans had called the team for decades.

Officially, the Washington Senators were the Washington Nationals, and team materials reflected the official name. Brotman recalls asking the team's graphic artist, Zang Auerbach, if there was a way to animate the Nationals on the cover of the yearbook.

Auerbach, brother of legendary basketball coach Red Auerbach, responded, "Nothing. It just lays there."

"How about Nats?" Brotman asked.

"Same thing," Auerbach said. "Nothing."

"Can you do something with Senators? Maybe an old-type senator, with a frock, where he throws the ball and catches it?" Brotman suggested.

"Yeah, I can do that with the Senators," Auerbach said.

Brotman says he ran the idea past Calvin Griffith, and the owner signed off. But the "Senators" didn't draw much better than the "Nationals." In fact, Washington was dead last in American League attendance for six straight years leading to the team's move to Minneapolis in 1961.

When the new Senators moved into D.C. Stadium in 1962 (later renamed RFK), there were more bad teams—and more small crowds. Only once did the expansion Senators finish in the top half of the league in attendance, but that was also the team's only winning season—1969.

Ben Walker, longtime lead baseball writer for the Associated Press, grew up in the Washington area and has a bittersweet memory of the All-Star Game that year. Eleven years old at the time, Walker, his parents, and his best friend, John, arrived at RFK Stadium early for the game.

"Neither John nor I had ever seen a National League player in person," recalls Walker, now AP's deputy sports editor. "We'd seen color pictures of them, of course, from when my dad brought home the *Street & Smith's* magazine at the start of the season. But we didn't have a color TV and could only imagine how they'd look for real. Funny thing: As much as John and I were eager to see Willie Mays and Hank Aaron and Bob Gibson, we really, really wanted to see Chris Cannizzaro. He was San Diego's lone All-Star representative, and we couldn't wait to look at those mustard-brown Padres uniforms that everyone was talking about."

That year's All-Star Game epitomized the sport's increased offense, thanks to a lowering of the pitcher's mound. In 1968, the National League had won the Midsummer Classic, 1–0. Walker experienced firsthand the harder hits in 1969:

"Now the game starts and the ball is flying. The NL leads 9–3 after four innings and already there have been five home runs. And then comes the hardest hit of the day. To me, anyway. I was eating popcorn when Johnny Bench hooked a hard foul into the third-base seats, a few rows behind us. I turned my head and—whack!—got bonked squarely on the forehead by the carom.

"The ball zinged back onto the field, where third-base coach Leo Durocher picked it up and tossed it into the crowd. A few minutes later, a young man brought the ball over to me while several fans poured out their Cokes, grabbed napkins and put together makeshift ice packs. With a bump forming on my head, my mom is worried and wanted me to see a doctor; my dad figured I was fine and wanted me to see Pete Rose. We stayed and to be honest, I don't recall much else about the game. That might be because there wasn't a whole lot of action after that, and it ended up 9–3."

The Senators drew 918,000 fans that year, second-highest in Washington baseball history to that point, and the most ever by the second Senators team. But attendance plummeted the next two years, bottoming out at 655,000 fans in 1971, the team's final year in Washington. Overall, the Senators II finished last in league attendance four times in 11 years. That track record gave Major League Baseball pause before it agreed to bring a team back to Washington for a third time. But Senators players say the fans had a bad rap.

"How many times will you go see a horseshit movie?" asks Tom McCaw, who was the first baseman on the 1971 Senators team and the batting coach for the new Nats. "Now, if you're a horseshit ball club, do you expect people to come out eighty times a season and support you? No, you wouldn't do that. You still need to be entertained. If you're a bad ball club, and if you've been a bad ball club for several years, people aren't going to go see it. If we're going to be an entertaining ball club—and I think we will be—we will have no trouble drawing people in Washington over the years."

Former Senators slugger and fan favorite Frank Howard says that baseball held onto the old perception of Washington as a small, southern, sleepy town.

"I don't care if you're in Battle Creek, Michigan, or Minneapolis-St. Paul, the aura of having major league baseball lasts two to three years," he says. "The aura of having a new stadium lasts two to three years. But this is America—we love a winner. And you've got to be competitive. You can't ask the public to buy an inferior product."

"I wouldn't trade the seven years I had here in Washington," he adds. "You talk about courtesy and respect accorded to an individual—it was unparalleled. I appreciate it. The fans were very supportive. Not that they didn't boo me all the time. It's like Don Zimmer used to say, 'You're an amazing man. They're either all for you or all against you. You strike out four times, you got everybody in the house coming down on you. You hit a home run, everybody's giving you a standing ovation.'

"That didn't bother me. It's all part of it. One guy said he'd eat his hat if I hit a home run. I hit a home run, and he started chewing on it. The fans here were great."

Former shortstop Eddie Brinkman says that although few fans came out to see the Senators, he enjoyed the ones that did.

"Some came just to scream at us—which was fine," he says. "You pay your money, you can yell anything you like. One guy used to always sit by the third base dugout, and he'd get on me all the time. We called him Red Dog because he had red hair. He called me a hamburger—'You hamburger, you bum, you stink!'"

"Red Dog" would bring his cooler of beer and come to every game, Brinkman recalls.

"We loved it," he says. "Then in 1969, when I started to do a little bit better, one day I walk out of the dugout and I hear, 'Hey Brinkman!' I turn around and it's Red Dog. 'You're pretty good.' And I said, 'Red Dog, you son-of-a-gun, you're always getting on my butt, now you're going to come over here and kiss my rear end? Get out of here. Get back over there and get on me some more. I don't want to talk to you."

Joe Dempsey says he's excited about Washington's new team, but he's having a hard time with the name.

"For some reason 'the Nationals' just can't come out," he says. "I still, through senility I guess, want to say Senators. Nats? I couldn't do it before! If you grew up in Washington and played ball, you were constantly swarmed by gnats, those little teeny no-see-ums that would find their way into your eyes and ears! No, I'm just going to call 'em the Senators. Everybody will know who I mean. It's a generational thing, I guess, just like my blue cap with the Red block 'W.'"

TEN

THE WASHINGTON NATIONALS: BASEBALL RETURNS

THE WASHINGTON NATIONALS: BASEBALL RETURNS

On Sunday, October 3, 2004, the Montreal Expos suited up for their final game as a Canadian team. In an odd bit of historical symmetry, the finale was held at the same place the team had played its first game in back in 1969—Shea Stadium in New York. That location didn't keep fans from Canada from making the trip across the border to see off the team, with some rooters sporting jerseys and caps of old Expos stars such as Gary Carter and even Randy Johnson, who began his career in Montreal in the late 1980s.

Four days earlier, 31,000 fans had come out to watch the Expos' final home game, a 9-1 loss to the Florida Marlins. Had the Expos drawn those kinds of crowds consistently, they would have stayed in Montreal. But the team pulled in just 750,000 fans for the season, dead last in baseball, averaging around 9,400 fans.

In their first game in '69, the newborn Expos had raced out of the starting gate with an 11-10 victory over the Mets, that year's world championship team. But in 2004, Montreal sputtered to an inglorious end, falling to New York, 8-1, in its final game. Fans behind the visitors' dugout chanted "Let's Go Expos" in the ninth inning, but Montreal failed to rally for any runs. Expos starter John Patterson took the loss, surrendering four runs in 4⅓ innings. The team finished with a 67-95 record, barely over .400, last in the National League East.

"I've seen this with some other ball clubs when they were moving, and from a distance it doesn't really hit you," Expos manager Frank Robinson said. "But when you're involved in this thing and it's final—the name Montreal Expos won't be in existence next year, that's a rude awakening, and it's a sad situation because of the people it's going to touch in a negative way."

That's a sentiment with which Washington baseball fans could identify. Twice, they had their team yanked away—in 1961, when the Senators left for Minnesota, and again a decade later, when the second version of the Senators left for Texas. Now, they were finally benefiting from a team move, as the Expos were on their way to Washington.

On the same day as the Expos home finale, September 29, Major League Baseball had announced that the team would be relocating to the nation's capital—the first team move since the Senators became the Texas Rangers after the '71 season. Washington stood out among a field of relatively weak competitors for the Expos: Las Vegas, Portland, Oregon, and Norfolk, Virginia. The stiffest challenge came from the Washington suburb of Northern Virginia.

Michael Hinckley delivers to the plate for the new Washington Nationals in Spring Training. (Photo by Doug Pensinger/Getty Images)

"Congratulations," Commissioner Bud Selig told Mayor Anthony A. Williams, who had led the effort to bring the team to Washington. "It's been a long time coming."

In a statement, Selig called Washington one of the world's most important cities. "There has been tremendous growth in the Washington D.C. area over the last thirty-three years," he said, "and we in Major League Baseball believe that baseball will be welcomed there and will be a great success."

That view represented a change-of-tune for a sport that had kept Washington at arm's length for three decades. Many owners saw the city as a two-time baseball loser that couldn't support a team, and the opposition of Baltimore Orioles owner Peter Angelos resonated with his fellow monopolists in baseball's ownership cabal. Angelos argued that a team in Washington would take fans away from the Orioles, thirty-five miles away. In fact, despite the announcement, Angelos was still not on board, and it would take several months to come up with a deal to prevent him from suing to block the move.

But Congressman Tom Davis, a Republican who represents a suburban Washington district in Virginia, says that Congress would not have tolerated baseball keeping the Expos out of Washington because of Angelos.

"We made it very clear that if baseball bypassed this, and went to some place like Norfolk, that there would be a problem," says Davis, who held highly-publicized hearings on steroid use among professional athletes in 2005. "Because we were clearly the right marketplace."

"Republicans hate Angelos," Davis adds. "He's given a lot of money to Democratic candidates. There was just no way we were going to let Angelos hold this up. I think at the end of the day there would have been a reaction to that, on top of the steroids hearings."

Washington Post sports columnist Tom Boswell says that by 2004, baseball in Washington had become an inevitability.

"This is something that had to be done," he says. "The Washington market is enormous. You can't ignore it. You can't allow the owner of one team to operate as a monopolist and prevent an enormous market from getting a team. You can't have a Ford dealership in Baltimore but not allow them in Washington. So this had to happen. But I will be far happier if it works out well for both cities, for both franchises."

Because of the city's commitment to build a new stadium for the Expos, the deal also needed city council approval, which would prove to be far more challenging than initially thought, despite the support of a majority of council members at the time.

The baseball owners were blown away by the city's generous offer—a publicly funded $440 million stadium on the Anacostia riverfront, to be paid for by taxes on the city's largest businesses, ballpark concessions, and team rent. (That price tag would swell to $535 million by the next year.) They also realized that Washington was not the deteriorating, riot-plagued town it had been back in the early 1970s. Instead, with its fast-growing suburbs, the Washington region was one of the most affluent in the nation.

The Expos came to Washington without a single owner—or more to the point, with twenty-nine of them. The owners of the other teams had purchased the Expos in 2002, and had run the franchise on a shoestring budget and barnstorming act's schedule. The Expos played 22 "home games" in Puerto Rico in both 2003 and 2004, adding thousands of miles of travel, which took its toll on the players.

The team's name was another uncertainty. "Washington Expos" was never really on the table; the name just didn't fit. Many old-time fans, as well as Selig, favored the name Senators, in tribute to the old Washington teams. But Mayor Williams argued that because the city had no actual voting representation in the Senate (or the House for that matter), the team shouldn't be called the Senators. He favored the Grays, the name of the old Negro League team that was based in Homestead, Pennsylvania but played many of its home games in Washington in the 1930s and 1940s. A third choice: the Nationals, as bland as the Grays, but with an equally compelling historical justification. Washington's old team was known formally as the Nationals until 1956, although fans usually referred to them as the Senators.

A *Washington Post* poll in early November, 2004, found that 40 percent of local fans surveyed favored Senators; 14 percent liked Nationals; and 10 percent preferred Grays. The rest had no preference or had some other name in mind (Bureaucrats?). In the end, the Nationals emerged as the consensus choice.

"The Mayor was on Grays," said team President Tony Tavares. "Bud was on Senators. I think you see a compromise candidate. But I don't want to sell it as that. I think it's a great name."

On November 9, the Washington City Council added some suspense to the team's move by delaying a vote on the stadium deal. That stall came after three stadium opponents won elections to the city council, although they would not take office until the following January. Fueled by a backlash against giving hundreds of millions of dollars in public subsidies to millionaire baseball owners to field a team of millionaires, critics argued that the money would be better spent on the city's schools and other pressing needs. Proponents countered that the stadium would help promote economic development in a part of the city that badly needed it, and that much of the money would come from taxes generated by the team.

Meanwhile, MLB moved ahead with the relocation. On December 3, the owners formally approved the team's move to Washington, 29-1, with only the Orioles' Angelos voting no.

But less than two weeks later, the City Council threw a high, hard one at the owners, voting to require that at least half the cost of the new ballpark be covered by private money. When Major League Baseball balked at the legislation, it appeared that the Expos' move to Washington could fall through. Baseball owners were furious, believing the City Council had pulled a bait-and-switch.

"The legislation approved by the District of Columbia City Council last night does not reflect the agreement we signed and relied upon after being invited by District leaders to consider Washington as a home for Major League Baseball," said MLB President Bob DuPuy in a statement. "The legislation is inconsistent with our carefully negotiated agreement and is wholly unacceptable to Major League Baseball."

The sport stopped all promotional activities for the team, including a press conference scheduled for that week to show off the Nationals new uniform. MLB also closed the team store and offered refunds to fans who had put down deposits for season tickets. A sense of doom pervaded the city's baseball fans, who realized if baseball pulled out of the deal, there surely would not be another chance to get a team.

But a week later, negotiations involving City Council Chairman Linda Cropp, who had pushed for the private spending provision, Mayor Williams, and baseball officials salvaged the deal. The compromise called for the city to seek private funding for half the cost, but did not require it; and for the city and Major League Baseball to share the cost of insurance to cover overruns on the new stadium. MLB agreed to drop the penalty that Washington would pay for failing to open the stadium by 2008, from $19 million to $5.3 million. The City Council barely passed the new deal, 7-6. Essentially, one vote preserved baseball in Washington.

"Take me out to the ball game," fans sang in the council chambers after the vote. "Finally and at last, all of us have risen above the fray," Williams said, "and the Washington Nationals are rounding third and heading for home. Isn't that great?"

City Councilman Jack Evan, the driving force on the council for the baseball deal, says he never thought the deal was in danger.

"I knew we had the votes to get it done," he says. "Going into the baseball process, I knew the activists and the anti-baseball people were going to be against it, because they always are."

With the politics finally resolved, at least for the upcoming season, the Nationals could finally focus on putting players on the field. The team, which had finished 14th in the National League in runs scored in 2004, had already made a few off-season moves in an effort to improve its lineup. First, the Nats' aggressive new general manager, Jim

Bowden, signed two free agent players to fill out the left side of the infield—third baseman Vinny Castilla and short-stop Cristian Guzman.

Castilla hit 35 home runs in 2004 and led the National League with 131 RBIs, although he produced those numbers in Denver's hitting-friendly mile-high atmosphere. Guzman, a good defensive shortstop, hit .274 in Minnesota. But both players became huge disappointments for Washington.

Guzman and Castilla rounded out an infield that featured two productive but injury-prone players on the right side, first baseman Nick Johnson and second baseman Jose Vidro.

Next, Bowden traded for talented but temperamental right fielder Jose Guillen, sending the team's leading hitter, right fielder Juan Rivera (.307 in 2004) and shortstop prospect Maicer Izturis to the Anaheim Angels in the deal. Guillen had hit .294 with 27 home runs and 104 RBIs with the Angels in 2004, but the team suspended him late in the season after Guillen, angry at being lifted for a pinch runner, threw his helmet toward manager Mike Scioscia.

And in January, Bowden solidified the starting pitching rotation by signing Esteban Loaiza as a free agent. Loaiza, a 21-game winner with a 2.90 ERA in 2003, had slumped badly in 2004, finishing with a 5.70 ERA, but he would turn things around in 2005.

In February, the Nats finally debuted their new uniforms, as Guillen, Guzman, starting pitcher Zach Day and closer Chad Cordero met with fans and the media in the delayed dress rehearsal. Guillen indicated he would try to keep his infamous temper in check in his new city.

"I just have to learn to be a political man," he said. "I think I'm in the right town to start learning that."

On March 2, the Nationals played their first game ever, winning 5-3 over the New York Mets on a cool, sunny day at Space Coast Stadium in Viera, Florida. Although just a Grapefruit League exhibition, the contest had the trappings of a playoff game. ESPN broadcast it on national television, and the game attracted a hundred members of the media and a sellout crowd.

The ballpark sported the old teal seats from the Expos era, but the team played in brand-new Nationals uniforms—crisp, out-of-the-box white with red lettering. Guzman got Washington's first hit, a line drive up the middle, and Guillen slammed the first home run, muscling a ball over the right-centerfield wall.

The Nationals entered spring training enthusiastic about their new home.

"It's very exciting for the team to be here," catcher Brian Schneider said in a conversation before the team's first spring game against its new regional rivals, the Baltimore Orioles. "To get a chance to play here, to be part of the team that comes back to the nation's capital is very, very special. I'm glad that the city could get a team. I know they've wanted it a long time."

Schneider, whose family is from Annapolis, just 30 miles from D.C., said that Washington was the right fit for the team.

"I know toward the end of the Senators, attendance was down, and the team was down a bit, but sometimes it takes someone losing something to really appreciate it," said Schneider, a top-flight defensive catcher and clutch hitter. "They lost a team, and they wanted baseball back so much, and the ticket sales obviously shows that they're ready for a team."

The starting rotation appeared deep, featuring Livan Hernandez, Tony Armas Jr., Tomo Ohka, John Patterson, Day and Loaiza, and the Nationals also had a tough young stopper in Cordero. But the hitting was thin, despite the off-season acquisitions. The team struggled to find the right fit for the top of the lineup, deciding to shunt off its center fielder and leadoff man, Endy Chavez, to the minor leagues after Chavez struggled to get on base during spring training. Two months later, the team traded Chavez to the Philadelphia Phillies for outfielder Marlon Byrd.

Washington went back to left fielder Brad Wilkerson as its leadoff man, a miscast role for a man who had hit 32 home runs in 2004. But his excellent .374 on-base percentage made him the default choice. Rookie Ryan Church took over for Chavez in center, with Guillen playing right field.

"I think we have a chance to contend this year," manager Frank Robinson said as he surveyed his team in the spring. "I'm not saying we are contenders. I'm saying we can contend, compete on a daily basis with any team in this league."

"There's an eagerness here for this ball club to finally step forward, step up, and for people to stop feeling sorry for ourselves and let's show people that this is a good organization and we have good talent," he added.

Before the Nationals played their first regular-season game, Major League Baseball inked a deal with Orioles owner Peter Angelos that embittered many Washington fans. For years, Angelos had blocked a team from moving to the city, claiming the nation's capital as part of his territory. Now, to placate the litigious Orioles owner, MLB announced a new Mid-Atlantic Sports Network that would broadcast Nationals games but give the Orioles the profits. The Orioles owned 90 percent of the network, and MLB, as owners of the Nationals, owned the rest. The deal wasn't totally one-sided; the new network would pay the Nationals $21 million a year in broadcast fees.

Still, the arrangement helped reinforce perceptions in Washington that MLB was willing to sacrifice the new team's profitability and future success to block an Angelos lawsuit. Making things worse, Comcast, a cable company that broadcast the Orioles games, got into a legal battle with Angelos and refused to air the Nats games on its system, leaving millions of Washington-area fans without access to the majority of the team's televised games.

A few days later, on April 4, 2005, the Nationals and their fans put aside regional rivalries and politics to mark a momentous occasion: the team's first regular-season game. Although the Nats started their season on the road in Philadelphia, the 2½-hour drive tempted hundreds of Washingtonians to skip work and head north to see the rebirth of Washington baseball.

The Nats' starting pitcher, workhorse Livan Hernandez, didn't make it past the fifth inning, and Washington fell behind 7-1. By the seventh, the Nats had pulled to within 7-4, and Terrmel Sledge, who had homered in the previous inning, came up with the bases loaded and a chance to give Washington the lead. But he bounced into a rally-killing double play, and Washington lost, 8-4.

The Nationals rebounded from the loss to win five of their next eight games on the road trip, and came home amid much fanfare with a 5-4 record and a tie for first place in the National League East. The team's home opener on Thursday, April 14 against the Arizona Diamondbacks, was the hottest ticket in town, as lobbyists, lawmakers, celebrity journalists, and lawyers jockeyed for the choicest seats in the sold-out stadium.

Washington's Senators, including Diamondbacks fan John McCain, were on hand to see the old Washington Senators, such as Frank Howard, Eddie Brinkman, and Mickey Vernon, take their positions at RFK in a generational passing of the torch. The Nationals' starting players trotted out to their positions to receive their gloves from their baseball ancestors.

President George W. Bush revived an old local and national tradition by throwing out the first ball, but the president's appearance came at a cost. As Bush made his toss, and even as the game started, thousands of fans in the sellout crowd languished outside the stadium, trapped in long lines waiting to go through metal detectors installed for the presidential security. Once inside, fans forked over cold cash for cold dogs after waiting for forty minutes in concession stand lines.

Still, the return of baseball on a beautiful April evening inspired far more celebration than carping. "Ladies and gentlemen," welcomed Charlie Brotman, the former Senators public address announcer, "the moment you've all been waiting for for thirty-four years, let's meet your 2005 Washington Nationals!"

At 7:06 p.m., starting pitcher Livan Hernandez wound up and fired the first pitch in Washington Nationals history. The fastball sailed past Arizona's Craig Counsell for a strike, making a loud pop as it snapped into catcher Brian Schneider's mitt. The ball was sent to the Nats' dugout, a short stop on its way to the Baseball Hall of Fame in Cooperstown, New York. A few pitches later, Hernandez struck out Counsell looking, and the crowd erupted in thunderous cheers.

Baseball may have undergone an offensive explosion during its absence from the nation's capital, but the hitters offered no evidence of that through the first few innings at RFK. When the Nats came to bat in the bottom of the fourth, it was still a scoreless game. Castilla, the reigning RBI champion, came up with Guillen and Vidro on base, and crushed the ball the other way, into the right-field corner, for a two-run triple. Fans throughout the stadium jumped up and down, and the old stadium rocked. The Nats made it 3-0 when Schneider drove Castilla home with a sacrifice fly.

Two innings later, Castilla widened the lead to 5-0 with a home run into the Washington bullpen, then came out of the dugout for the Nats' first curtain call. Castilla, who had doubled in the second, now needed just a plain old single to hit for the cycle. In the eighth, he came up with a chance to accomplish the feat. But Diamondbacks reliever Lance Cormier drilled him, and Castilla reluctantly walked down to first base, as the virgin Nationals fans booed angrily.

Lest those fans get too spoiled by an easy win, the Nats made things interesting in the ninth inning. Protecting a 5-0 lead, Hernandez walked Luis Gonzalez and surrendered a single to Shawn Green—just the second hit by the Diamondbacks all evening. Chad Tracy followed with a three-run homer to right field, and now it was a ballgame.

Manager Frank Robinson took out Hernandez, who tipped his cap to acknowledge a standing ovation as he walked to the dugout. The team's 23-year-old stopper, Chad Cordero, came in to try to put the game away. He quickly got the second out, bringing cheering fans to their feet. But the next batter, Quinton McCracken, singled to center, and the dangerous pinch-hitter Tony Clark came to the plate as the potential tying run. The six foot seven inch slugger sported a .538 batting average in the young season. Clark swung and made good contact with the ball, driving it to centerfield, but not deep enough at cavernous RFK. Church corralled the ball for the historic victory, and the aging ballpark lit up with fireworks and photographic flashes.

"Words can't describe it," Church told reporters after the game. "I've never been in a World Series, but I've seen some on TV. And that atmosphere, that crowd noise—it seemed just like a World Series."

The moment provided a cathartic antidote to the last major league game at RFK, played in 1971 as the Washington Senators were about to move to Texas. With two outs in the ninth inning and the Senators leading the New York Yankees, 7-5, fans swarmed onto the field. Play could not resume, so the Senators were forced to forfeit the game—their 96th loss in yet another abysmal season.

Washington fans had no rational reason to expect anything better from their new team. After all, the Expos had finished with nearly as many losses in 2004 (95), and despite some off-season upgrades, most experts picked them for last in the National League East in 2005. True, it was only April, but Washington's home opener victory put the team into sole possession of first place, with a fat .600 winning percentage. And the Nationals would prove they had contending power well beyond April.

On May 19, the Nationals climbed five games over .500 with a 3-2 victory over the Milwaukee Brewers, as Livan Hernandez improved to 7-2. The team then left for a 10-day road trip that almost knocked them out of the race. Washington went just 2-7 against Toronto, Cincinnati and St. Louis and returned home on May 30 a .500 team.

Worse, Washington faced the two best teams in the division upon its return—the Atlanta Braves and Florida Marlins. The Braves had a chance to bury the upstarts in a crucial four-game series. Instead, the Nationals won three of four, including two games by one run each. In the finale, the Washington bullpen blew a 3-2 lead in the eighth inning, surrendering four runs. Trailing 6-3, the Nats rallied for five runs in the bottom of the frame to pull off an improbable 8-6 victory, thanks to backup catcher Gary Bennett's three-run double. With the victory, Washington pulled within 1½ games of the Braves and Marlins, who were tied for first place.

Next up were the Marlins. No problem. Washington won the first two games of the series to leapfrog over Florida, but still trailed the Braves by ½ game. The next day, Sunday, June 5, the Nationals accomplished something that hadn't been done in seventy-two years—a Washington team in first place this late in the season. The last time it happened, the Washington Senators were on their way to the 1933 pennant. The 2005 Nationals did so by coming from behind for the fourth straight time, overcoming a 2-0, seventh-inning deficit against tough Florida pitcher A.J. Burnett on their way to a 6-3 victory. Washington took over sole possession of first place with Atlanta's 5-2 loss to Pittsburgh.

"You couldn't ask for any more than we've done in the first seven games against these two ball clubs," Robinson told reporters after the game. "These were tough ball clubs. They were leading this division. For us to come up and stand up and pull down the wins against them, it's a good feeling."

Incredibly, the Nationals won their next six straight, to extend their winning streak to 10 games and wrap up a 12-1 homestand. In 11 of the victories, the Nats came from behind to win. As they exchanged high-fives on the field following their 10th straight victory, a 3-2 win over Seattle, fans gave them a standing ovation—and some players applauded back. The 37,000 fans on hand that day deserved it just as much. They had catapulted the Nats' attendance to 1,056,642, breaking the single-season Washington attendance record set in 1946. And it was only June 12.

With the victory, Washington improved to 37-26 and a baseball-best 24-9 at home. They left home with a 1 ½-game lead over the second-place Philadelphia Phillies. They then won five of nine in a tough road swing through Anaheim, Texas and Pittsburgh, maintaining their hold on first place. When they came home, the Nationals won five of six games in the final week of June to cap an unbelievable month of baseball. Washington went 20-6 in June—a .769 winning percentage.

"That's a tremendous year, or month, I'm sorry," Robinson said after the Nats defeated the Pirates, 7-5 on June 30, completing a three-game sweep. "After the last three years, it seems like a year. That's a tremendous month, and the players deserve an awful lot of credit for the way they have performed and the way they have handled things. They just keep going out and doing the job."

Washington's victory over the Pirates, the team's 15th win in its last 16 games at RFK, improved the Nats' home record to 29-10. Chad Cordero saved his 15th game of the month, tying a major league record.

The Nationals' performance transfixed a city that had been without baseball of any kind for three decades, and without a legitimate pennant contender for far longer. Crowds of 30,000 or 35,000 routinely came out each night, tripling the typical attendance for the old Senators teams.

The Nats continued to confound the baseball world by going to Chicago and sweeping a three-game series against the Cubs. In the finale, Washington blew a 2-0 lead in the ninth and a 4-2 lead in the eleventh, but won the game on Brian Schneider's twelfth-inning home run. Cordero snapped a string of 26 straight saves by blowing the ninth-inning lead.

The victory gave the Nats a 50-31 record at the midpoint of the season, a .617 winning percentage, and a 5½-game lead in the National League East. The team was on pace to win 100 games. If this seemed way too good to be true for a team that had lost nearly 100 games the year before, well, it was.

Things went south just as the second half of the season began, and on a day that should have been a natural for a Washington team—the Fourth of July. The Nats looked like they were on their way to another low-scoring victory, taking a 2-0 lead against the New York Mets into the seventh inning behind the pitching of John Patterson.

But Patterson tired in the seventh, giving up a single and double, and reliever Louis Ayala surrendered two more hits, allowing both runners to score and the Mets to tie the game. Then New York rallied for three runs in the ninth against Sun-Woo Kim to pull out a 5-2 victory.

Although Washington beat Pedro Martinez the next night to even the series, the Mets took the final two games. Then the Nationals went to Philadelphia and lost two of three as they headed to the All-Star break.

Despite the rough week, the Nats were still in good shape at the break. They owned a 52-36 record, and a 2½-game lead in the division.

The question was: how were they were doing it? All year long, injuries had decimated Washington's lineup, taking chunks of the seasons of Jose Vidro, Jose Guillen, Nick Johnson, Brad Wilkerson and Ryan Church. Washington scored fewer runs than any team in baseball, was tied for last in homers, and had actually been outscored overall. But the Nats, dubbed "one-run wonders," were a staggering 24-10 in one-run games. Fans who subscribed to the law of averages knew that the team couldn't sustain that pace.

At the All-Star break, GM Jim Bowden picked up veteran lefthander Mike Stanton, two weeks after the Yankees had cut him, to help solidify the bullpen. More importantly, Bowden made an effort to upgrade Washington's listless offense by trading for Rockies outfield slugger Preston Wilson, dealing starting pitcher Zach Day and minor league outfielder J.J. Davis.

In the first half of the year, Wilson had batted .258 with 15 home runs and 47 RBIs, putting him on pace for nearly 30 homers and 100 RBIs for the season. But like Castilla the year before, Wilson had benefited from the inflationary effects of Denver's thin air. RFK offered hitters no such advantage. In fact, prompted by a *Washington Post* aborted surveying expedition, team officials re-measured the distances to the outfield wall, and found that the power alleys were 395 feet from home plate, not the 380 feet posted on the wall. That helped explain why RFK had been the stingiest home run park in the major leagues in the first half of the year.

But the midseason acquisitions didn't help, and the All-Star break couldn't stem Washington's recent slide. The Nats won just three of their first 11 games after the break, and Robinson decided to bench shortstop Cristian Guzman, whose

.189 batting average sat like an albatross on the weak Washington lineup. The team headed to Atlanta for a crucial three-game series on July 26. Washington's once 5½-game lead had vanished; the Nationals and Braves were now tied for first place atop the division.

Washington got a psychological boost when its injury-plagued opening-day infield started a game together for the first time since May 4. But the one-run magic that had carried the team through the first half of the season had evaporated. They lost the first game, 3-2, after Cordero blew a 2-1 lead in the bottom of the ninth inning. Atlanta won the game in the tenth when Andruw Jones walked with the bases loaded, and Washington was out of first place for the first time in more than a month.

Atlanta took the next two games of the series, 4-3 and 5-4, to complete a devastating sweep and drop the Nats three games out of first place. The baseball karma had turned on the team; Washington's losing streak in one-run games would reach an unlucky 13.

Still, the Nationals stayed in the hunt. They didn't play great baseball, but they rebounded from a terrible July to play around .500 in August. By the end of the month, they had fallen to last place despite having a winning record in the hypercompetitive Eastern Division. But more importantly, even if the division title was looking like a long-shot, Washington was in the midst of the wild card race.

As late as mid-September, the Nationals looked like they were going to make a strong run for the playoffs. They went to New York and swept a three-game series against the Mets, then extended the winning streak to four on September 16 by taking the opening game of a series in San Diego. With just two weeks left in the season, the Nationals had somehow remained contenders—only 2½ games out of the wild card lead.

The next night, the Nats took a 5-0 lead into the bottom of the ninth and appeared to be on their way to their fifth straight win. The Padres put a run across to make it 5-1, then Khalil Greene stunned the Nationals with a game-tying grand slam off Cordero, Washington's fourth pitcher of the inning.

Three innings later, Ramon Hernandez tagged Washington pitcher Jon Rauch for a three-run home run and an 8-5 Padres victory. The crushing loss dropped the Nationals 3½ games behind the Houston Astros in the wild card race.

The next afternoon, the final game of their six-game road trip, must have felt like a screening of *Groundhog Day* to the Nationals. Washington led 1-0 in the eighth inning, but Greene once again came through, this time in less dramatic fashion, with a game-tying sacrifice fly in the bottom of the inning. San Diego won the game in the ninth when

Washington reliever Joey Eischen threw errantly to first base after fielding a sacrifice bunt attempt, allowing Miguel Olivo to score the winning run. The second straight bullpen meltdown wasted a great performance by starter Esteban Loaiza, who had pitched seven scoreless innings. Now the Nats were 4½ games out and effectively out of the playoff hunt.

The Nationals returned home after those dispiriting losses to face the San Francisco Giants. Clinging to a 2-1 lead in the top of the ninth inning, Washington faced Barry Bonds with two outs and a runner on first base. Bonds had just returned the week before after missing most of the season recovering from knee surgeries, but he had smashed an upper deck home run earlier in the game. So Robinson told pitcher Livan Hernandez to pitch Bonds carefully, and Hernandez walked the Giants slugger on four pitches. The strategy backfired when Moises Alou followed with a three-run homer, and the Giants staved off a Nats rally in the bottom of the ninth to hold on for a 4-3 victory.

Those three late-inning collapses marked the final turning point of the Nationals' inaugural season. What could have been a seven-game winning streak heading into the final stretch turned into a three-game losing streak.

Washington was officially eliminated from the race a few days later, losing to the Mets, 6-5, at RFK, as New York completed a three-game sweep. The Nationals fell to an even .500 for the first time since May, and back into last place.

"In the second half, we collapsed," said catcher Gary Bennett. "Plain and simple. We didn't get it done."

With six games remaining, the Nats still had a couple of goals left: to finish over .500 and out of last place. After sweeping the Florida Marlins in a three-game series, that looked like a pretty good possibility. Not only were the Nats three games over .500 with three games to go, but they had pulled into third place, barely above the Marlins and Mets.

But the hungry Philadelphia Phillies, still alive in the wild card race, came to RFK and swept a season-ending three-game series. That dropped the Nats to a final record of 81-81, and dumped them to the bottom of the division. A .500 record would have been good enough for second place in the Western Division and a share of third in the Central, but that was small consolation to a team that had ruled the East for a good chunk of the summer.

"It would have been really a fairy tale if we could have pulled this thing off," Robinson said after the final game, a 9-2 loss to the Phillies. "They wouldn't have even touched this in Hollywood."

At the finale, the 36,000-plus fans gave the Nationals a standing ovation as the players took their positions, then applauded for more than five minutes after the final out. The players and coaches returned the favor by throwing hats, balls and other souvenirs to the fans. Robinson made a "No. 1" gesture to the fans.

"It was very special," the manager said. "Very special. The fans have been special all year long. They had a lot of feelings for this ballclub, and this ballclub had a lot of feelings for them. And without them, we wouldn't have had the season that we did have."

He might have said *seasons*, because the Nats really played two different mirror-image seasons in 2005. At the midway point, the Nationals played an over-their-head 50-31; from then on, they posted an underachieving 31-50 record. The team that at one point was 23-7 in one-run games finished 30-31 in such contests.

For fans of the old Washington Senators, the 2005 Nats offered some interesting historical parallels. The last time Washington got a new team, in 1961, it, too, had shocked experts early on, although not to the degree the Nats did. The '61 team started out 30-30, then collapsed over the last 100 games to finish in a tie for last place.

Guzman, who hit .219 only after a strong finish, was an echo of weak-hitting Senators shortstops. Eddie Brinkman hit .188 and .187 in back-to-back seasons in the late '60s, and the 1961 starting shortstop, Coot Veal, hit .202 with just eight RBIs in 218 at-bats that year.

While the rest of the Nats didn't struggle as badly as Guzman, the offense failed to offer much of a threat. The lineup had no .300 hitter, no slugger with 25 home runs, no 100-RBI man, not even one player with as many as 10 stolen bases. Nick Johnson led the team with a modest .289 batting average, and Jose Guillen paced the team with 24 home runs and 76 RBIs. Brad Wilkerson walloped an impressive 42 doubles, but he hit just .248, and his 11 home runs at cavernous RFK marked a huge drop-off from 2004, when he had hit 32.

The Nationals finished last in the league in hitting (.252), home runs (117), runs (639) and slugging percentage (.386). But that wasn't nearly as awful as the 1960s Senators teams, who hit .227, .231, .228, .234, .223, and .224 in a six-year period from 1963 to 1968.

And the 1945 Senators would have killed for 117 home runs. That team hit just 27 round-trippers all season, and just one all year at home, but still managed to finish in second place.

The 2005 Nats also continued a tradition of former Hall-of-Fame players running the team as manager. Ted Williams, like Frank Robinson, exceeded expectations in his first year in Washington, guiding the 1969 Senators to a winning record before the team tanked in subsequent seasons. Although the 2005 Nats had a poor finish, they still improved by 14 games over the 2004 Expos.

The Nationals had other accomplishments to point to in 2005. Stopper Chad Cordero led the National League with 47 saves, and his 1.82 ERA paced a Nats pitching staff that posted the fourth-best ERA in the league (3.87). Relievers Hector Carrasco, Luis Ayala, and Gary Majewski all had ERAs under 3.00. Several starters had good years too, including John Patterson (9-7, 3.13), Esteban Loaiza (12-10. 3.77), and Livan Hernandez (15-10, 3.98).

But the most impressive statistic was the team's attendance: 2.7 million. Only 10 teams drew more than the Nationals, despite a television deal that shut out many fans and a late start in marketing the team. The Nationals averaged 33,728 fans per game in an outdated ballpark.

The main accomplishment, of course, was having a team at all. For most of the 20th century, Washingtonians enjoyed the rhythm of a baseball season: the reliable company of a radio broadcast on the front stoop; a relaxing evening stretched out on the couch in front of the TV, perhaps dozing through the fourth inning; watching the flight of a ball at a game against a blue afternoon sky or starry night; checking the box scores in the next day's newspaper. A generation of Washington fans never got to experience those pleasures. Perhaps a century from now, the three decades without a team will merit only a footnote in a proud 200-year Washington baseball tradition.

BIBLIOGRAPHY

ARCHIVAL SOURCES

The Historical Society of Washington, DC

The Library of Congress, Washington, DC

Martin Luther King Jr. Memorial Library, Washington, DC

National Archives & Records Administration, College Park, MD

ARTICLES

Ceresi, Frank and Carol McMains. "The Washington Nationals and the Development of America's National Pastime." *Washington History* 15.1 (2003): 26-41.

Considine, Bob and Shirley Povich. "Old Fox: Baseball's Red-Eyed Radical and Archconservative, Clark Griffith" (first of two articles). *The Saturday Evening Post* 13 Aug. 1940: 14–15, 127–134.

Considine, Bob and Shirley Povich. "The Old Fox Turns Magnate: Baseball's Red-Eyed Radical and Archconservative, Clark Griffith" (second of two articles). *The Saturday Evening Post* 20 Aug. 1940: 18–19, 91–98.

Dowling, Tom. "The Uncensored Ted Williams." *Washingtonian* March 1970: 36–39, 56–60.

Eisele, Al. "Bob Short: This Fast-Talking, Short-Tempered Promoter from Minnesota Is Not Likely to Keep Cool in the American League Cellar." *Washingtonian* March 1969: 46–47, 65–69.

Fimrite, Ron. "Sam Lacy: Black Crusader; A Resolute Writer Helped Bring Change to Sports." *Sports Illustrated* 29 Oct. 1990: 90.

Griffith, Clark as told to J. G. Taylor Spink. "Doesn't Sigh for 'Good Old Days' Return: Points to Game's Progress, Sees Balance Achieved in Pitching and Slugging." *The Sporting News* 23 July 1952: 11–12.

Griffith, Clark as told to J. G. Taylor Spink. "Sale of Son-in-Law Cronin 'Nats' Financial Salvation': Owed Bank $124,000 at Time, Griffith Reveals; Decided on Big Deal 'for Good of Joe and Mildred.'" *The Sporting News* 30 July 1952: 11–12.

Lieb, Frederick G. "Griffith Canny as Hill Star, Pilot, Owner: Always a Battler, He Helped to Build A.L. as Major." *The Sporting News* 2 Nov. 1955: 11–14.

Small, Collie. "Baseball's Improbable Imports." *The Saturday Evening Post* 2 Aug. 1952: 28–29, 88–90.

BOOKS

Brashler, William. *Josh Gibson: A Life in the Negro Leagues.* New York: Harper & Row, 1978.

Cobb, Ty with Al Stump. *My Life in Baseball: The True Record.* Garden City, NY: Doubleday & Co., 1961.

Gilbert, Bill. *The Seasons: Ten Memorable Years in Baseball and in America.* New York: Kensington Publishing Corp., 2003.

Hartley, James R. *Washington's Expansion Senators (1961–1971).* Germantown, MD: Corduroy Press, 1998.

Judge, Mark Gauvreau. *Damn Senators: My Grandfather and the Story of Washington's Only World Series Championship.* San Francisco: Encounter Books, 2003.

Kerr, Jon. *Calvin: Baseball's Last Dinosaur.* Dubuque, IA: Wm. C. Brown Publishers, 1990.

Mantle, Mickey and Herb Gluck. *The Mick.* New York: Jove Books, 1986.

Mead, William B., and Paul Dickson. *Baseball: The President's Game.* Washington, DC: Farragut Publishing Company, 1993.

Povich, Shirley. *The Washington Senators.* New York: G. P. Putnam's Sons, 1954.

Ruth, Babe as told to Bob Considine. *The Babe Ruth Story.* New York: E. P. Dutton & Co., 1948.

Snyder, Brad. *Beyond the Shadow of the Senators: The Untold Story of the Homestead Grays and the Integration of Baseball.* Chicago: Contemporary Books, 2003.

Stuart, Jeffrey Saint John. *Twilight Teams.* Gaithersburg, MD: SARK Publishing, 2000.

Thomas, Henry W. *Walter Johnson: Baseball's Big Train.* Washington, DC: Farragut Publishing Company, 1995.

INTERVIEWS

Bosman, Dick. Personal interview. April 2005.

Boswell, Tom. Personal interview. March 2005.

Brinkman, Eddie. Personal interview. April 2005.

Brotman, Charlie. Personal interview. April 2005.

Davis, Tom. Personal interview. April 2005.

Dempsey, Joe. E-mail interview. May 2005.

Durenberger, Dave. Personal interview. May 2005.

Fankhauser, Henry. Telephone interview. August 2005.

Farley, Jack. E-mail interview. April 2005.

Gilbert, Bill. Telephone interview. April 2005.

Gildea, Bill. Telephone interview. April 2005.

Grzenda, Joe. Personal interview. April 2005.

Hannan, Jim. Personal interview. April 2005.

Hardage, Robert. E-mail interview. May 2005.

Hochberg, Phil. Personal interview. March 2005.

Holdforth, Bill. Personal interview. April 2005.

Howard, Frank. Personal interview. May 2005.

Kennedy, John. Telephone interview. April 2005.

Kuhn, Bowie. Telephone interview. May 2005.

McCarty, William. Telephone interview. April 2005.

McGaw, Tom. Personal interview. March 2005.

Schneider, Brad. Personal interview. March 2005.

Sievers, Roy. Personal interview. April 2005.

Solomon, George. Personal interview. March 2005.

Valentine, Fred. Personal interview. April 2005.

Vernon, Mickey. Personal interview. April 2005.

Walker, Ben. E-mail interview. July 2005.

Wills, Maury. Telephone interview. April 2005.

Wolff, Bob. Telephone interview. April 2005.

Yost, Eddie. Telephone interview. April 2005.

BIBLIOGRAPHY

NEWSPAPERS/WIRE SERVICES

The Associated Press
Los Angeles Times
New York Sun
New York Times
Washington Afro-American
Washington Daily News
Washington Post
Washington Star
Washington Times
Washington Times-Herald
Washington Tribune

NIXON TAPES (FROM NATIONAL ARCHIVES & RECORDS ADMINISTRATION)

President Nixon on White House telephone with Robert H. Finch. 22 Sept. 1971, 6:55– 6:57 p.m.
President Nixon in Oval Office with Stephen B. Bull, Walter E. Washington, Jerry V. Wilson, John D. Ehrlichman, and Egil G. "Bud" Krogh Jr. 13 Oct. 1971, 11:06 a.m.–12:02 p.m.

WEB SITES

Baseball Almanac. 2005. http://www.baseball-almanac.com/.
Baseball Library. 2005. http://www.baseballlibrary.com/.
Baseball Reference. 2005. http://www.baseball-reference.com/.
Baseball Hall of Fame. 2005. National Baseball Hall of Fame and Museum. http://www.baseballhalloffame.org/.
Retrosheet. 2005. http://www.retrosheet.org/.

OLD SENATORS STATISTICS

Year	League	Record	Finish
1960	American Lg	73–81 (.474)	5
1959	American Lg	63–91 (.409)	8
1958	American Lg	61–93 (.396)	8
1957	American Lg	55–99 (.357)	8
1956	American Lg	59–95 (.383)	7
1955	American Lg	53–101 (.344)	8
1954	American Lg	66–88 (.429)	6
1953	American Lg	76–76 (.500)	5
1952	American Lg	78–76 (.506)	5
1951	American Lg	62–92 (.403)	7
1950	American Lg	67–87 (.435)	5
1949	American Lg	50–104 (.325)	8
1948	American Lg	56–97 (.366)	7
1947	American Lg	64–90 (.416)	7
1946	American Lg	76–78 (.494)	4
1945	American Lg	87–67 (.565)	2
1944	American Lg	64–90 (.416)	8
1943	American Lg	84–69 (.549)	2
1942	American Lg	62–89 (.411)	7
1941	American Lg	70–84 (.455)	6
1940	American Lg	64–90 (.416)	7
1939	American Lg	65–87 (.428)	6
1938	American Lg	75–76 (.497)	5

Year	League	Record	Finish
1937	American Lg	73–80 (.477)	6
1936	American Lg	82–71 (.536)	4
1935	American Lg	67–86 (.438)	6
1934	American Lg	66–86 (.434)	7
1933	American Lg	99–53 (.651)	**AL 1**
1932	American Lg	93–61 (.604)	3
1931	American Lg	92–62 (.597)	3
1930	American Lg	94–60 (.610)	2
1929	American Lg	71–81 (.467)	5
1928	American Lg	75–79 (.487)	4
1927	American Lg	85–69 (.552)	3
1926	American Lg	81–69 (.540)	4
1925	American Lg	96–55 (.636)	**AL 1**
1924	American Lg	92–62 (.597)	**WS 1**
1923	American Lg	75–78 (.490)	4
1922	American Lg	69–85 (.448)	6
1921	American Lg	80–73 (.523)	4
1920	American Lg	68–84 (.447)	6
1919	American Lg	56–84 (.400)	7
1918	American Lg	72–56 (.562)	3
1917	American Lg	74–79 (.484)	5
1916	American Lg	76–77 (.497)	7
1915	American Lg	85–68 (.556)	4
1914	American Lg	81–73 (.526)	3
1913	American Lg	90–64 (.584)	2
1912	American Lg	91–61 (.599)	2

Year	League	Record	Finish
1911	American Lg	64–90 (.416)	7
1910	American Lg	66–85 (.437)	7
1909	American Lg	42–110 (.276)	8
1908	American Lg	67–85 (.441)	7
1907	American Lg	49–102 (.325)	8
1906	American Lg	55–95 (.367)	7
1905	American Lg	64–87 (.424)	7
1904	American Lg	38–113 (.252)	8
1903	American Lg	43–94 (.314)	8
1902	American Lg	61–75 (.449)	6
1901	American Lg	61–72 (.459)	6

NEW SENATORS STATISTICS

Year	League	Record	Finish
1971	AL East	63–96 (.396)	5
1970	AL East	70–92 (.432)	6
1969	AL East	86–76 (.531)	4
1968	American Lg	65–96 (.404)	10
1967	American Lg	76–85 (.472)	6
1966	American Lg	71–88 (.447)	8
1965	American Lg	70–92 (.432)	8
1964	American Lg	62–100 (.383)	9
1963	American Lg	56–106 (.346)	10
1962	American Lg	60–101 (.373)	10
1961	American Lg	61–100 (.379)	9